TRANSFORMED

God has a destiny for your life

Brian Gingles

WestBow
PRESS
A DIVISION OF THOMAS NELSON

WestBow Press books may be ordered through booksellers or by contacting:

WestBow Press
A Division of Thomas Nelson
1663 Liberty Drive
Bloomington, IN 47403
www.westbowpress.com
1-(866) 928-1240

ISBN: 978-1-4497-9034-9 (sc)
ISBN: 978-1-4497-9033-2 (e)

Library of Congress Control Number: 2013906040

Printed in the United States of America.

WestBow Press rev. date: 4/8/2013

"And we, who with unveiled faces all reflect the Lord's glory, are being transformed into His likeness with ever-increasing glory, which comes from the Lord, who is the Spirit."

(2 Corinthians 3:18, NIV)

TABLE OF CONTENTS

INTRODUCTION: IS CHANGE NECESSARY AND POSSIBLE?

As a young man I was never interested in religion. By religion I mean the external traditions and trappings that most faiths, including Christianity, develop. I was, however, very interested in the possibility of a spiritual reality, which always seemed just out of my reach. In my more thoughtful moods, before I became a Christian, I would ask myself three searching questions. All three questions have, I suspect, concerned every human being on this planet, at some point in their lives.

The first question sounds simple but has profound implications. I sometimes wondered, "Is there a God?" Is there an all-mighty, all-knowing Divine Being who has a plan for humanity and who is in ultimate control?

The second question was both personal and universal. It was this, "How can I become a better person?" All of my attempts at self-improvement ended in frustration and disappointment. New Year's Resolutions seldom lasted beyond January! Permanent, meaningful character development seemed frustratingly impossible.

The third question, which combines elements of the first two, was this, "Is there any meaning or significance to my existence? Is there more to life than eating, drinking, sleeping and waking?" Dared I believe that I, and every other human being, might have an eternal and significant purpose?

Having discovered the answer to the first question I attempt in this book to explore the Bible's answers to the second and third. The following chapters record my own journey of discovery, aided by the truth of God's Word and the wise counsel of the Holy Spirit. You, the reader, will be delighted to share my joy and wonder at affirming that there is a loving, gracious God who has an amazing plan for our lives and who has both the desire and the ability to transform us into something infinitely better than we were when we first came to Him!

Picture a butterfly chrysalis. You would scarcely believe that something so beautiful and free as a butterfly could spring forth from something so ordinary and restricting. Now, picture your own life. It may be even harder to believe that your inner self might be transformed – even by the power and grace of God. Dare we believe that we could become spiritually transformed into His workmanship, into people full of light, purity, freedom, beauty and power? And can we believe that God has an even more astonishing plan for us than merely improving on the desperate person who gladly grasped His offer of salvation? How could you or I ever fulfil God's stated plan for us, to become the "likeness" of Jesus? The Bible makes such a promise and if it is indeed true, as I am convinced that it is, then how can God perform this astonishing work in us?

Our transformation can only begin when we personally accept the truth and power of the words of Christ[1]. What is the truth about individual transformation, as taught by the Bible? The New Testament provides the answers, and we will explore these in detail throughout this book. The Old Testament also contains promises of personal, individual transformation, as it anticipates the ministry of the Messiah, Jesus Christ. One example of these Old Testament promises is expressed in Isaiah 61:3. Here we are encouraged to accept that we need not be permanently shaped by our sinfulness, by genes or by negative circumstances; rather we can be transformed by God for His glory:

"To appoint unto them that mourn in Zion, to give unto them beauty for ashes, the oil of joy for mourning, the garment of praise for the spirit of heaviness; that they might be called trees of righteousness, the planting of the Lord, that he might be glorified." [2]

Although there is a specific context to these promises (*"them that mourn in Zion"*) there is nothing in this passage that is not promised repeatedly, throughout the Bible. Indeed, Jesus quotes these words at the beginning of His ministry, as His divine manifesto. These promises are made by God to the individual – Jew or Gentile – who seeks God through salvation in Christ with all of his or her heart. God's promise to such a person is this: you provide the ashes and He will transform them into something beautiful, for His glory. This is Good News!

It is said that when the master sculptor looks at a block of stone he already sees in it the statue or carving that he will create. We may look like unpromising blocks of stone in our own eyes but when the Master Craftsman looks at us, He already sees Christ formed within us! He sees us not just as we are but as we will be. You may struggle with faith for yourself but God has no difficulty in believing that He can transform you, if you are willing.

As we shall see, God has guaranteed your ultimate transformation into the likeness of Christ, in His divinely inspired book, the Bible. Search it for yourself to see the wonderful promises He is making to you. I have now followed Christ for over thirty years and, to my great joy and excitement, I have observed – in my own life and in the lives of others – the miraculous transformative power of these promises made real in believing individuals by the work of the Holy Spirit. In a world full of empty claims, Christianity, when wholeheartedly lived and faithfully applied, works! Any promise of any kind is only effective when backed up by the means to make good on it. When we believe that the promises of the Bible have all the weight, authority and resources of heaven behind them we can stake our lives and our eternal destinies on them.

Since becoming a Christian in October 1978 I have experienced first hand the power of God, moulding me more and more into His *"workmanship"*[3]. Anyone who knows me will confirm that this process is not yet finished! But it is my confident hope that He who has begun a good work in me will complete it. And He can do the same for anyone who puts their full trust in Him. As well as the evidence of my own experience, I have also counselled many Christians during more than thirty years of ministry. I have been thrilled to witness the power and effectiveness of the truths explored in this book, as precious individuals and couples have faithfully embraced them and applied them to their lives. Christ is never a disappointment when sought earnestly and humbly.

As we begin to explore this hope for personal transformation, some questions are natural. What is God's goal, His creative vision for us? And how will He transform us? Why does He want to transform us? How long will it take? Can we play a part in this process? I seek in this book to communicate – as clearly and faithfully as I can – my understanding of the biblical answers to these questions which, when answered with genuine faith in God's truth, can bring amazing changes to our lives.

Chapters 1-4 seek to answer the questions posed earlier. What is God's goal for us, as He changes us? Why and how does He do this? How long will it take? Can we play a part in this process? Chapter 1 answers the question: what is God's plan and purpose for humanity? Chapter 2 presents us with the necessity for change, and how God has provided for it. Chapter 3 considers how God heals, transforms and renews the wounded heart. Chapter 4 explores God's plan for our minds – a much neglected subject. Chapter 5 goes on to discuss some of the main ideas, influences and beliefs that lead many away from the knowledge of God and therefore, away from the hope for genuine and lasting transformation. Chapter 6 considers the part we are to play in this process of transformation. Chapter 7 seeks to answer the question: what is God's prototype for our eventual transformation? Chapters 8 and 9 consider the glory of God and the effect of Christ's Second Coming on us.

In each chapter I try to give practical approaches and biblical answers for the reader. There are also Study Questions as well as References and Notes at the back of the book, for those who wish to use it as a stimulus for discussion or for further study. I trust that all of these thoughts will aid your understanding of the path of truth: the path of Christian transformation.

I should add, at this point, that there is no substitute for prayer and the reading of God's Word, aided by the revelation of the Holy Spirit. Crucially, God's truth must not be seen as a formula - the "five steps to happiness" approach! Rather, the Bible repeatedly makes the point that the Holy Spirit reveals God's word to us and, as we apply this revelation persistently and steadfastly by faith to our lives – always allowing the Holy Spirit to help us - we will see fundamental changes take place. There is nothing dull or irrelevant about what the Bible promises you. As you believe in it and obey the leading of the Holy Spirit you will embark on the ultimate transformative adventure. Your life will never be the same again!

We must be patient with God and with ourselves. True and lasting change is always painful and costly, and it does not always come as quickly as we would wish! But do not despair, the ultimate goal is worth it all. As Jesus said, when we *know* the truth – really accept it and make it our own - *it* will make us free.

CHAPTER 1

SOME FOUNDATIONAL TRUTHS

In The Beginning

Our journey of discovery, in search of the answers to our questions, will assume as true the unique claims of the Bible. It is the only guide that is ultimately trustworthy. It is therefore the only text I have referred to in the body of this book. We must begin our search for the truth at the very beginning of human history. Why did God create man? And why did He create him to be and act as he did?

Creationism – the belief that God made the universe and all living things – including mankind – is a matter of faith. I am very aware that there are Christians who hold one of three general positions on the Creation story of Genesis. There are those who believe that every word of Scripture is to be understood literally, unless it is clearly a metaphor. If God is all-powerful, why could He not make the world and everything in it in six days? Then there are those who see the Creation story as part literal and part metaphorical where, for instance, time-scales are symbolic rather than literal. Before the Reformation, for example, some church fathers and leaders regarded the Genesis account as partly allegorical:

Augustine, to mention just one, spoke of the six days of creation as signifying categories of creation rather than a literal time-span. Finally, there are Christians who have a faith in God but who believe also that Genesis is entirely allegorical – that it is a pre-scientific account of something much more complicated, which is gradually being explained by science. My personal conviction is that there is overwhelming textual evidence that Genesis 1:1 – 2:3 is to be understood as literal, historical narrative. The Bible makes it clear when it is speaking poetically or allegorically; we are, otherwise, to understand it literally.

The Bible asserts that God created the heavens and the earth by the power of His word. By this same word of power (Hebrews1:3) He sustains the universe. The Bible itself gives us some clear guidance on how we are to understand the divine act of creation:

> *"It is by faith that we understand that the universe was created by God's word, so that what can be seen was made out of what cannot be seen."* [1]

The last part of this verse is open to some interesting discussion but two things are stated very clearly: that the material universe was created by God; and that, for the Christian of any period, faith works backwards in time as well as forwards. That is, the Creation story is a matter of faith just as much as the Second Coming of Christ is.

The same principle applies to the rest of the opening part of this chapter. God's dealings with Adam and Eve are understood by faith and revelation, rather than by human knowledge or understanding. The assumption of this writer is that Genesis was inspired by God to communicate key truths to mankind. These truths include His purpose for creation, the unique creation of man, the relationship God wishes to have with man, and the origin and nature of evil. In Genesis the "why" questions are more important than the "how" or "when" questions. I state this as one who is absolutely convinced of the inerrant Word of God.

God's Original Plan for Mankind

Genesis is the biblical book of beginnings. It describes man's creation and God's original and eternal purposes for humanity. The insights offered in Genesis are highly instructive for anyone who wishes to know the Christian view of *why* we were made. It also gives us a context for knowing *what* God wishes to make of us, as He transforms us.

We learn, in Genesis, that man was made to have intimate fellowship with God, his Maker. The biblical view of man is that he is a threefold being – that there are three distinctive parts or aspects to our beings. Each human being is made up of body, soul (mind, emotions, will) and spirit. There are many significant overlaps, among and between these three aspects of human identity, but it does help our understanding to consider them separately. Adam was given a body so that he could exist in a material, physical universe. He was given a soul with which he could express worship and grow in his understanding and knowledge of God[2]. Adam was also given a spirit with which he might relate to God, who is Spirit[3].

> *"Then the Lord God took some soil from the ground and formed a man out of it; He breathed life-giving breath into his nostrils and the man began to live"* [4]

We see here that, physically, man was created out of the same substance as the earth around him but that God then breathed His own breath (or spirit)[5] into man to cause him to live, spiritually as well as physically. This life was to be lived in harmony with God and with the material, physical universe – over which he was to be steward[6]. In the New Testament we see an explicit reference to the threefold nature of man:

> *"May the God who gives us peace make you holy in every way and keep your whole being – spirit, soul*

*and body – free from every fault at the coming of
our Lord Jesus Christ."* [7]

Not only does this verse communicate a clear recognition of man's threefold nature, it also gives expression to God's desire, as stated by Paul, to redeem and transform each aspect of each human being. God's desire for you, as a redeemed individual, is the life-long sanctification (the setting aside of worldliness and an increasing conformity to a godly nature) of your body, soul and spirit, preparing you for your full redemption in Christ. This redemptive plan will lead to an eternal destiny spent with Christ. It necessitates and enables a process of constant change within the believer.

Before we consider life, let us first look at how death entered the human experience. After the description of man's creation Genesis goes on to describe man's fall from grace. The serpent tempted Adam and Eve by sowing seeds of doubt in their minds about God's promises and sanctions. The wily serpent's weapons were scepticism, doubt and deception:

> *"The snake replied, 'That's not true; you will not
> die. God said that, because He knows that when
> you eat it you will be like God and know what is
> good and what is bad'."* [8]

It is interesting that the devil lured Eve with the very temptation by which he fell: for in his pride he too had wanted to be like God. It is interesting to note, also, that the serpent equates divinity with knowledge (rather than holiness, or love, or any of the other divine attributes). The next verse indicates that there was a sensual attraction in the form of a lure of the senses and the soul towards this tree; the tree was "beautiful" as well as offering the intellectual appeal of "knowledge". Eve was fatally tempted in body, soul and spirit. She gave way to temptation, which then led to sin. She also persuaded an irresponsible Adam to share in this sin. The consequences of this vanity were catastrophic for man and for the rest of creation.

What were the consequences? God had said that eating the fruit of knowledge would result in death. Physically, man continued to exist but was punished by banishment from the presence of God, the source of all life. Furthermore, man's body became mortal and vulnerable to illness. Man's soul gained knowledge, at the direct expense of losing purity and an open relationship with God. This newfound knowledge brought guilt, shame and misery to Adam and Eve with the result that their innocence "died". God's light went out in man's life and man now lived in spiritual darkness. It was in his spirit that man most immediately experienced death. In 1 Peter 3:4 we are told that the spirit of man "*is not corruptible*" but what died was man's relationship with God – his spirit was rendered "dead" because of trespass and sin so that his ability to have an intimate spiritual relationship with a holy God was utterly destroyed. The only means by which he could now communicate with God was by external religious observance, by attempting to please God through futile, outward acts.

What did man gain? He acquired a knowledge of the good he could no longer do, and he acquired a knowledge of evil – all kinds of ideas and myths that extended and developed the very doubts and deceptions first inspired by Satan. All pathways of deception and error began with these first acts of disobedience and they all keep alive the vanity that human knowledge is superior to the knowledge of God. I believe that because of his success in Eden the devil still exploits human pride and love of forbidden knowledge, with the goal of persuading men and women to deny the truth of God. Interestingly, this identifies the mind rather than the body as the principal target for temptation. Mankind is still listening to the lies of the serpent.

> "*As soon as they [Adam and Eve] had eaten [the fruit], they were given understanding and realised that they were naked…they hid from [God] among the trees*" [9]

What a tragic transformation of man! Changed from living in a state of innocence, shamelessness and rapport with God, Adam and Eve were now reduced to wretched, spiritually "dead", embarrassed and corrupted beings, pathetically hiding from God in the very trees over which they had originally been given dominion. How sad God must have been! However, He was not taken by surprise, for His plan of redemption had already been formed. Nevertheless, He was surely grieved by the foolishness and self-destructiveness, the sinfulness, of His creation.

In His great love, God had already prepared an atonement for this sin and a way by which man might be restored to all the benefits that Adam and Eve enjoyed before the Fall (the chief benefit being an open relationship with a holy God as the spiritual Father of mankind). Actually, in Ephesians 2:4-7, Paul makes it clear that salvation through Christ is superior to Adam's innocence because Christ's atonement demonstrates the amazing grace of God:

> *"But God's mercy is so abundant, and His love for us is so great, that while we were spiritually dead in our disobedience He brought us to life in Christ. It is by Christ's grace that you have been saved. In our union with Christ Jesus He raised us up with Him to rule with Him in the heavenly world. He did this to demonstrate for all time to come the extraordinary greatness of His grace in the love He showed us in Christ Jesus."* [10]

You and I owe God a great debt of love. He who has been forgiven much, loves much!

This pathway of redemption back to God had to overcome a number of obstacles created by the Fall. One problem was judicial: the righteousness and justice of God demanded grave punishment for sin. Another problem lay in the now corrupted nature of human beings. A holy and loving God, who had already planned to "buy back" mankind, also planned to change sinful, fallen man's nature – an apparent impossibility!

Some of these issues are beautifully expressed in Psalms 101. This Psalm majors on the themes of loyalty and justice; it expresses the passionate desire of the writer to live a pure life that is pleasing to God. However, it also expresses, with great frankness, some of the difficulties of so doing. In verse 2 the Psalm expresses the intention of the writer but also his need for God's intimate and personal help to make possible these changes in his life,

> *"I will behave myself wisely in a perfect way [AB:*
> *"I will give heed to the blameless way"]. O when*
> *wilt thou come unto me? I will walk within my*
> *house with a perfect heart."* [11]

In order to *"walk"* in God's blameless *"way"* with a *"perfect heart"* the individual needs an intimate relationship with God. The Psalmist's cry from the heart indicates his longing for God's presence as much as for personal integrity. Each believer must also allow the Holy Spirit to develop that inner determination whereby what is desired is not just a change of character but above all a deep, intimate relationship with the holy God of all grace.

The first question the reader must ask is, "Do I need to change?" If the answer is "Yes" then read on! Radical change implies both an inner transformation and a change of route – a change of direction for the pathway your life is taking. If the answer is "No" then you might like to ask your closest friend to confirm your own opinion of your perceived state of perfection! Better still, ask the Holy Spirit to show you if you are yet perfect in the eyes of God!

The next issue we will consider is how the individual choices we make form steps that take our lives in certain directions. Each choice is a step along life's journey. I do not believe that life is a meaningless, random set of events and experiences which lead us nowhere. The metaphor of the "pathway" speaks of purpose, of design and of a destination.

Paths Leading to Life and Death

Some time ago I looked more closely at a well known Bible verse:

"Thy word is a lamp unto my feet and a light unto my path." [12]

For years I had blurred the two statements into one: "*feet*" and "*path*" seemed to go together, as did "*light*" and "*lamp*". I could visualise the solitary shepherd on the still, dark hillside or the town dweller in the shadow of an alley, warily inching along unknown, dangerous routes using a constant personal light or lamp to avoid dangers or wrong turnings. However, when I looked more closely at this Bible verse I began to see two related yet distinct insights. The "lamp" for my "feet" refers to the step-by-step illumination and guidance for each decision in life. This illumination is provided by the revealed truth of God, which is often described as "light" in the Bible. Light is promised for the believer for the minute, detailed, daily, personal guidance we all need as practising Christians. Moreover, the "light" for your "path" illumines large sections of the path you will take when following God. It lights up the future as well as the present.

A path can be any roadway we take in order to reach our desired destination. It is a pre-determined way to be taken and a way which others have taken before us. It is a well-trodden route. For each this path represents a unique journey but the individual does not invent it. Christ's path has existed for many centuries and multitudes have chosen to take it. In the same Psalm the writer asks God to enable him to:

"Make me go in the path of thy commandments…" [13]

It is obvious that here the word is used as a metaphor, using the image of a path to represent a set of beliefs, commandments and ideas. These fundamental beliefs and ideas shape the direction in which we travel through life. We take a path, meaning we make choices based on what we believe and value. As we travel through life, these beliefs and values will determine how we act. The path has a destination as well as a beginning and will involve a journey. The writer of this Psalm asks God to enable him to stay on the path of God's commandments.

A brief study of the biblical uses of the word "path" reveals that the word is used in a number of key ways. Often God's commandments – or consistent obedience to them - are described as keeping to a *"straight"* path, whereas false teachings, or a way taken in disobedience to God's teaching, are described as *"crooked"* or *"wide"* paths. A number of Scriptures express relevant prayers of supplication, asking God for help to walk His path. The key to choosing His "path" lies in the willingness of the individual to obey God's directions for his or her life and, thereby, follow His pre-determined path. In Hosea 2:6 the word "paths" is used to indicate the choices of someone wishing to run away from God. We each have a free will and sometimes we exercise it foolishly. The writer of Hosea gives us a model prayer to frustrate the plans of this wilful backslider, *"she [Gomer] shall not find her paths"*[14]. Perhaps this might inspire each of us to pray a similar prayer for someone we know?

In Isaiah 59:7 *"run"* portrays the impulsive and driven nature of men gripped with evil desires, who take impetuous "steps" – a series of hasty but calculated individual actions or decisions, made by individuals intent upon following a path which leads to deception and ruin for themselves and others:

> *"Their feet run to evil, and they make haste to shed innocent blood; their thoughts are thoughts of iniquity; wasting and destruction are in their paths."* [15]

Here *"paths"* suggest busy thoroughfares – many travel this way and ultimately pay the price for doing so!

God has determined your path[16], desiring that it should lead to eternal life[17] and that its route should be characterised by peace[18]. What wonderful promises! God's path of truth is a path of righteousness, peace and joy in the Holy Spirit[19] and its destination is eternal life in Him.

One more biblical use of the word "path" is of particular interest to those who hope for transformation. In Hebrews 12:13 insight is given into the healing nature of God's path:

> *"And make straight paths for your feet, lest that*
> *which is lame be turned out of the way; but let it*
> *rather be healed.."* [20]

Here, again, there is an aspect of choice. We have a responsibility for making "*straight*" paths for our feet. If we do not our lameness (our inner weaknesses) will quickly send us off in the wrong direction. But if we continue to "walk in the Spirit" we will stay on the straight path and we will be made whole. The healing (of more than feet and legs!) is done by God but our part in this process is to remain on His path. This is achieved by deciding each day to obey God's revealed will. Transformation, as a consequence, is ultimately attained by a combination of God's grace and our faith and obedience.

Ways and Bents

Some aspects of my own character which have been most resistant to change have been my ingrained habits. These existed in my mind and heart like the grooves on an old-fashioned record. When I became a Christian some of these were dealt with quickly, some took years to overcome, and yet others are still being changed. Habits become so much a part of us that we come to see them as aspects of our personalities. God wants to replace all negative habits with positive ones. He wants to go even deeper, by dealing with the root causes that created these habits in the first place.

When we look a little more deeply into the English word "way", we gain insights that combine notions of obedience, paths and human nature; links that we have already begun to explore. A "way" can be a path*way* – literally, a well-trodden route linking a point of departure with a destination. As we have seen, a "path" or "way" can also be a biblical metaphor, a word picture for a route we take through life – a set of values and ideas that take us in a certain direction. "Way" can also be used to mean an individual's manner, for example, we might say that so-and-so has a "pleasant *way* with them". It can mean someone's "bent" or tendency. For example, what we do in an emergency tends to reveal our "way" of coping with problems. Those who are familiar with the game of Lawn Bowls will know that each bowl has an in-built bias, which tends to veer it off a straight line to the right or to the left. I'm sure we can apply the analogy to our own lives! What is your particular "bent"? You discover what it is in a crisis! For example, you may panic, or worry, or become self-pitying? If your reaction in an emergency is anything less than complete trust in God, ask Him to help you to change.

In Job Chapter 23, we gain an insight into how the word "way" can indicate a character trait that needs to change. In the midst of his great trial, Job asked God a series of very natural questions. His questions included: "Why is this happening to me?" and, "How long will this last"? Have you ever asked questions like this? It seems to me that all Christians have asked them at some time – repeatedly, perhaps – as a result of our inability to make sense of what is happening to us and around us. Job's conclusion is one of faith, hope and revelation – despite (or is it because of?) his appalling circumstances:

> *"He knoweth the way I take; when He hath tried me, I shall come forth as gold."* [21]

Here, the word *"way"* is a translation of the Hebrew word *derek*, which can mean a road, a course of life, or an habitual personality trait. Job realises that there is, within his character, an habitual response that must change (self-pity, or fear, or self-righteousness or self-justification?). God, knowing Job's "bent", designed a trial that would test Job in order to transform his character to *"gold"*. Note that the *"gold"* is already there, waiting to be purified and exposed by the heat of the trial.

So the word "way" has a number of possible meanings. There are two significant interpretations of "way" that are most relevant to the themes of this book. Firstly, a "way" can be a metaphorical route or road, a set of values and ideas outside yourself, which you have believed and internalised – causing your life to go in a certain direction. Secondly, "way" can be an internal habit, a personality trait, or a tendency that God may want to improve, alter or eradicate.

The pathway we follow must be chosen carefully, for it will lead to death or to life. As we travel this pathway – if we are open to God – He will change the internal "ways" that might otherwise cause us to deviate from God's true path. Changing our "ways" forms a significant part of the transformation of the Christian disciple. As we shall see, moving from "hearing about" God to "seeing" Him[22] involves deep and sometimes painful changes – alterations to our hearts, minds and spirits. When we see God more clearly we see ourselves as we are.

Walking in God's Path

In addition to the many references to "paths" and "ways" which appear in the Bible we also need to consider the corresponding metaphor of "walking". If the "path" is God's pre-determined route for your life (for which He has provided the Bible as a road map and the Holy Spirit as a guide) - and the "way" can be either a set of beliefs or an aspect of character - then to "walk" in obedience to God represents the step-by-step decisions we make in life, which take us towards our final destination. The Bible is full of references to "walking" as a picture of active faith and obedience. God will never force us to change but he does require a lifetime of active co-operation with Him, born out of faith, submission and humility.

One example of this use of "walking" is found in Romans 8:1, which famously begins with God's "not guilty" verdict on the individual who is saved by God's grace through faith in the atonement of Christ. Paul continues by stating the on-going condition of this promise and the evidence of its genuineness; he says that the true believer will *walk not after the flesh, but after the Spirit*[23]. So the genuine disciple of Christ will have a changed character, lifestyle, motives and behaviour.

He or she will live in and seek to please the Spirit, putting to death and considering dead their own fallen natures.

This picture of a lifetime of learning from the Holy Spirit and of being changed by Him is entirely consistent with the view of salvation and discipleship expressed throughout the New Testament. Salvation begins with an individual experience called the "new birth" but it also involves a process, a lifetime of transformation and dedication. Righteousness is no longer an impossibility but it is now made possible because God considers the Christian disciple to have Christ's righteousness. He also begins the process of transforming us, as we "walk" in obedience to Him. A constant series of choices is implied here. Every day the true Christian must consciously choose to walk God's way, conscious of the fact that this cannot be done without the help of the Holy Spirit, and His transformative power. No matter how far you feel you are from God just one step in His direction is a step in the right direction. He will meet you more than half-way: as you draw near to Him, He promises to draw near to you. The passage in Romans previously quoted goes on to deal with the role of the mind, after which Paul makes a powerful statement:

> "So then they that are in the flesh cannot please God."[24]

Logically, this would include anyone who is currently *"in the flesh"*. If anyone wishes to please God they must continue to dwell in the Spirit and walk in the Spirit. Two alternative ways of "walking" are presented to us by Paul, and two destinations are implied. One is a path that leads to death, the other is a path that leads to eternal life. Jesus identifies Himself as the light by which we walk. The light is a Person. He promises to light our paths and, as our Good Shepherd, to illumine even the darkest experiences of life[25].

Do You Want to Change?

"Do you want to change?" is one of the most important questions you could ever be asked, or ask yourself. It was one of the greatest obstacles to my acceptance of Christ as Saviour and Lord. I did not particularly like myself but radical change seemed a scary prospect! Your answer to this question will determine how you respond to God's gracious offer of help. I will attempt to explain how He can help in Chapters 2-4. But first, I would like to consider the attitude that is necessary for all lasting change.

No one changes until and unless they are convinced of three things: that change is necessary, desirable and possible. Someone once told me that no one ever turns away from a mirror until they are satisfied with what they have seen. The opposite actually seems to be more true: before the many real and mental mirrors in our lives, human beings seldom turn away satisfied with the image they have just seen before them. Sometimes this is because of a lack of self-esteem, or because of a profound rejection, or some other negative experience or attitude. It can also be, for the Christian, the lack of a full appreciation of the love of God for His adopted children. However, this dissatisfaction with who we are may also be because God is holding up His mirror to our lives to convict us of the need for change.

There is something inside us all that tells us that we need to improve. Look in any bookshop in any Western airport and you will see shelves full of books on self-improvement. We have all, at some time or other, longed for radical changes to our thinking, behaviour, character, spirituality or personality. And we have all been frustrated with the futility of our own efforts to make these changes happen. Eastern cultures are also familiar with the many promises of individual transformation and enlightenment made by all their major religions and philosophies. The desire for inner transformation would appear to be at once individual and universal, transcending all cultures and faiths. The conclusion for the Christian must be that God has deposited this desire for transformation in each human heart. No one wants to remain as they are, unless they are blinded by complacency.

In this book, I argue that individual change is defined by God in terms of what needs to be changed, how, why and when? I also argue that individual change can only be accomplished with God's help, in His time and in His way. My contention is that the God who made us – and has a wonderful destiny for each person who follows Him, on His terms – is best placed to transform us into the likeness of His Son, for His glory. In our deeply secularised Western society these are profoundly radical statements! I will go on to argue that the Bible has much to say about God's desire, ability and resources for changing us.

The true pathway of change can only begin with a single, essential first step: new birth into Jesus Christ. This pathway of many "steps" then offers a lifetime of change, made possible by the humble co-operation of the individual with the continuing work of healing, deliverance and sanctification by the Holy Spirit. The Bible expresses this work of the Holy Spirit through many promises. These biblical promises of redemption, salvation, wholeness, renewal, sanctification and healing all provide hope for the transformation of the individual.

Consequently, the Bible's promises are regarded, throughout this book, as inspired, infallible, truthful, verifiable and eternally relevant. This should provide answers for any person who, in responding to my question, "Do you want to change?" has asked their own follow-up question, "How can I change?"

Practical Applications

How can we begin or continue to co-operate with God in the process of transformation? To give the reader further hope I could record many testimonies of former addicts and other apparently hopeless cases who, in my experience, became genuine Christians and, as a result, found themselves free, secure and positive contributors within their churches, families and societies. I will give some of these testimonies, including some of my own, throughout this book. For the moment, let us consider some essential first steps to permanent and radical change.

The Bible exhorts us to believe and act upon some fundamental truths:

"No one can please God without faith, for whoever comes to God must have faith that God exists and that He rewards those who seek Him." [26]

These truths (faith in God's existence and in the trustworthiness of His promises) are essential to Christian transformation. Unless you are prepared to believe that God exists, that He loves faith (not arrogance!) and that He rewards those who persistently seek Him, then none of the rest of this book will be of any help. Whatever our need is we must believe that God exists and that He is who He says He is. We must also believe that His promises are eternally true and that they apply to anyone who believes. So, the Bible makes it clear that the *means* of change is the human response of faith to God's revealed truth. It is faith – not formulae - that opens the doors of our lives for God to do His work in us.

An excellent example of this process is outlined by Paul in Ephesians 3:14-19. In this passage Paul prays for something the Christians in Ephesus obviously did not automatically receive at their conversion. He prays that they would receive power to understand the nature and extent of the love of God for each believer. Here revelation, faith and confidence in God's love are seen as transformative – resulting in the believer being *"filled with the very nature of God"*. Although we do not rely on emotion and sensation as judges of what is true, nevertheless this love of God that changes us is experienced within the believer's heart and is held as truth in the renewed mind.

I remember praying for one lady at a Christian conference a number of years ago. She told me that – despite having been a committed Christian for years – she had never experienced the love of God. As we prayed, the Holy Spirit released the reality of God's experiential love into her heart. She was whooping, laughing and crying simultaneously and occasionally shouted, "I feel it"! What a joy it was to witness this transformation from theory to reality. This experience of God's love is very personal but it is a gift of God's grace for every believer, who asks and receives.

In terms of "light" (revealed truth), "walking" (a series of life-changing decisions based on obedience to God's will) and "paths" (a direction for your life determined by your beliefs and values), the key is obedient faith. If we are serious about allowing God to lead, guide and change us we must make Him Lord as well as Saviour of our lives. This implies a life of dedicated submission and humility, which views "full" salvation not merely as a single step but rather as a process that is costly and very blessed. The New Testament speaks about disciples, not mere converts (although every true convert will become a disciple). True discipleship is a better "path" or "way" than trusting in our own intellects to weigh up, then decide upon our chosen course or plan for our lives. Stubborn independence is an attitude fundamentally at odds with biblical discipleship. We are all guilty, at times, of thinking that we know better but the Bible says:

> "Trust in the Lord with all thine heart; and lean not unto thine own understanding. In all thy ways acknowledge Him, and He shall direct thy paths." [27]

If we follow this advice we shall walk in the light, along the pathway God has planned for us. We may make a few, temporary, deviations from it but we will always come back to the centre of God's will, drawn by His grace and love.

Finally, beware of any tendency that leads you away from God; appealing to the inherent pride in you that says, "I know better". The Bible is eternally relevant and true; it is a more certain compass than our feelings, or the ideas that have gained temporary currency in the world around us. We must put our faith in the author of the Bible and beware the cynics and doubters who would mock us out of our freedom in Christ.

CHAPTER 2

THE NECESSITY FOR CHANGE AND GOD'S GRACIOUS PROVISION

"Fools say to themselves, 'There is no God'. They are all corrupt, and they have done terrible things; there is no one who does what is right. The Lord looks down from heaven at human beings to see if there are any who are wise, any who worship Him. But they have all gone wrong; they are all equally bad. No one of them does what is right, not a single one." [1]

There was no one more surprised than I was when, on that October evening in 1978, I put my faith in Christ as my Saviour. I had been taken to a Christian service in Portadown (Northern Ireland) by my longsuffering Christian friends, on a Friday evening. I well remember muttering to myself as I entered that alien environment, "They're not going to get me!" To my eternal delight, I could not have been more wrong.

It was, in part, due to my friends' prayers and their witness – along with a sermon that seemed preached just for me – that I was brought to salvation. But what really shook me to the core, as the evening wore on, was the amazing and undeniable fact that I began to feel the tangible presence of the God I had not believed in. I realised that it was He who was communicating with me. I knew that my life could never be the same again. In seconds my entire view of God and of the meaning of my life changed completely and permanently. God had well and truly "got" me!

The process I went through that evening, to my enduring joy, is described in this chapter. But before joy could come I had to experience the sober realisation of my absolute need for salvation.

What a damning picture of humanity we see in the quotation at the beginning of this chapter. This vision of man, after the Fall, describes us all as naturally vain, wicked and antagonistic towards God. When anything is viewed from another perspective, it can look very different. The quotation from Psalms 14 offers us God's view of human behaviour and character. From a human perspective at least some people, some of the time, may appear morally good and kind. But from a holy God's perspective all men are entirely foolish, corrupt and morally blind, when measured against God's standards. According to the Bible man is too proud to acknowledge and worship his Creator and no one is capable of doing good, in God's eyes. The commonly expressed sentiment, that so-and-so would make a "good Christian" is at odds with what the Bible teaches. The biblical description of man portrays him as corrupt, selfish and morally blind. How could such a creature realise that he needs to be transformed, much less find a way to accomplish this apparent impossibility?

This is the first obstacle to transformation. Man lives in such a state of moral and spiritual darkness that he is in perpetual denial – incapable of seeing, much less agreeing with, the heavenly perspective mentioned above. In fact the initial response of most people to God's view of sin and fallen human nature is to become angry or defensive. Satan wants to keep us all in this state of angry, deceived ignorance:

> "*the God of this world has blinded the eyes of the unbeliever.*" [2]

19

The writer of Psalms 73:2 observes the apparently inconsequential blindness of the wicked. At first, he is dismayed by their apparent prosperity, well-being and health. The writer admits at first to being envious and explains its effect on his faith:

> *"But I had nearly lost confidence; my faith was almost gone because I was jealous of the proud when I saw that things go well for the wicked."* [3]

This can be a real problem for the follower of God. Why is God so kind to wicked people? In the New Testament, this problem is addressed by Jesus when He gives us an insight into God's amazing mercy and longsuffering. He teaches us that God makes the sun to shine and the rain to fall on the just and the unjust alike[4]. God's general, provisional grace benefits all of mankind. However, Paul, in Romans, has to say several times that we should not confuse divine mercy and patience with divine approval. Just because we are not being punished immediately does not mean that we are innocent, or that God does not see our sin. God gives us all opportunities to repent but ultimately a righteous God must judge sin.

The story continues in Psalms 73, verses16-17, which go on to give a very sobering reason why no one should envy the proud and wicked:

> *"I tried to think this problem through, but it was too difficult for me until I went into your Temple, then I understood what will happen to the wicked."* [5]

Here the Psalmist admits to something we can all agree on – these things are too hard for us to comprehend! We need help to see things from God's perspective. In order to gain His perspective, we must be in His presence, asking for His insight. It was only because of revelation that the psalmist saw the eventual doom of the wicked.

Another problem lies in our inability to judge moral issues as God does. It is difficult to understand why bad things happen to "good" people and good things happen to "bad". Part of the answer lies in Jeremiah 17:9, where *your* heart and *mine* are unflatteringly described by the prophet, inspired by God's Spirit:

> *"Who can understand the human heart? There is nothing else so deceitful; it is too sick to be healed."* [6]

Our hearts are not only the most corrupt things on this planet, they are also uniquely deceitful. Their judgements cannot be trusted. Furthermore, there is no hope, outside of God, for the human heart to be "*healed*". The prophet accepts that there is no human remedy for this condition. How, then, can we hope to see the need for improvement or have any hope for genuine and lasting change? The next verse begins to reveal the answer:

> *"I, the Lord, search human minds and test human hearts."* [6]

So, in both Psalms 73 and in Jeremiah 17, we are told that we need God's help to see ourselves and other people as He sees us.

The Epistle to the Romans, in the New Testament, is utterly honest and logical. It offers the clearest, most honest, description of the human condition that I have ever read. It begins by describing the complete inability of fallen man to do good, to please God or to glorify Him. Our natures are corrupt, it states, therefore all of our behaviour flows from a corrupt soul. Even our best attempts to do good are tainted. According to Paul the standard against which God measures our motives, thoughts and actions is not just the Law, given by God to Moses. Rather, God's ultimate standard of righteousness is Christ Himself. When our motives and actions are measured by God against this standard we are all found wanting – we are all condemned. Paul then speaks in Romans about four means by which God reveals to us the true nature of our sinful state and also the proofs of the existence of a holy God. Firstly, the Law of Moses convicts and condemns us. Secondly, creation demonstrates the existence of the Creator (whom we have failed to worship). Thirdly, our consciences prick us (but have been made insensitive through sinning). And fourthly, the Holy Spirit illumines our dark and sinful state. Paul is equally clear that all of mankind automatically stands condemned because we have all ignored these messages from God about our true pre-Christian condition. Such a state of wickedness and corruption cannot go unpunished by a righteous God. You and I need to be forgiven before we can be changed! This is a very unpopular message in today's secular, self-centred society, where each man considers himself to be the sole judge of his own conduct and the master of his own destiny.

When God's perspective on our natural condition is revealed to us the individual can experience and express all sorts of reactions. He or she might become defensive, angry, offended, confused or convicted. God gives grace to the humble, but He regards the proud from afar. He distances Himself from the proud. We must come to God on His terms, not ours. In order to do so we need the grace of God.

From the beginning to the end of this process of transformation, the grace of God is an absolute requirement for change to improve any of our lives. God then looks for faith, obedience and humility in us – a proper response to His gracious promises. This process of change begins with the acknowledgement that His perspective is the true one, the only one that ultimately matters. Without the grace of God we would not see the need for change. We would not see it as being necessary, desirable, or possible. How does God's grace make possible the process of transforming a sinner into a saint?

Grace

There are few more wonderful insights than the comprehension of God's grace towards us, undeserving, frail human beings. Every promise of God, every compassionate action of His – for our salvation, healing, deliverance, protection, provision and wholeness – depends on His grace. Every believer must grasp this truth: we are transformed not because we are good but because God is good.

The final words of Romans 2:4 state that it is:

"...the goodness of God [that] leadeth thee to repentance." [7]

The truth of the transformational significance of Christ's sacrifice on the cross can only be revealed to us by God. It makes no sense to the natural man. An individual's imperfection is revealed by an act of grace on God's part, or we would never repent to the living and holy God and thus receive forgiveness. And the act of divine forgiveness is purely based on grace, on the kindness and mercy of God.

The old definition of grace, "the unmerited favour of God", still serves us well. The word commonly translated as the English word "grace" in the New Testament is the Greek word *charis* which means: "God's gracious influence upon the human heart; deeming it acceptable as a favour; gift; liberality; joy". This Greek word is used 156 times in the New Testament, most frequently in Paul's letters. Grace is a foundational Christian truth but one that also needs to be held in correct balance against other central aspects of God's character and His dealings with man. Without the grace of God salvation and transformation would be impossible. Grace illumines our sinful condition and grace enables us to repent. The basis of our justification and salvation is the grace of God. Grace identifies (through the Holy Spirit) what needs to change and then enables us to be changed. Grace makes our on-going relationship with a Holy God possible and grace enables us to keep on being changed for the better. Grace is one of the key themes of the Bible, so the reader can look from Genesis through to Revelation and find that explicit or implicit examples of God's grace abound. This is because our God is a gracious God, full of compassion, love and mercy.

At the beginning of John's Gospel the apostle makes a number of telling comments about the grace of God in Christ. The word *charis* is used repeatedly in this passage (as well as similar English words like "gave"). One of these references to grace can be found in John1:17:

"For while the Law was given through Moses, grace — unearned, undeserved favour and

spiritual blessing — and truth came through Jesus Christ." [8]

The Law was and is holy, but it could neither redeem man, nor could it change him. Rather, the Law was intended to expose man's natural sinfulness, in much the same way that the traffic laws reveal our driving flaws. All any law can do is to expose wrongdoing and impose a penalty on it. Grace and truth have made a way to redeem man and to deal with the ingrained iniquity of each individual. In the previous verse (John 1:16), John makes it clear that grace is a repeated, lifelong gift. Because grace *"came through Jesus Christ"* those who are in Christ have constant access to grace. We receive grace for every occasion and we receive grace to enable us to *"walk in the light"*, being transformed as we go. Ephesians powerfully speaks of the unstinting grace of God:

> *"Which He lavished upon us in every kind of wisdom and understanding (practical insight and prudence),"* [9]

Learning how to receive God's limitless grace is vital for any disciple of Christ. In Romans 3:24 Paul makes it clear that grace is the only basis for salvation:

> *"All are justified and made upright and in right standing with God, freely and gratuitously by His grace (His unmerited favour and mercy), through the redemption which is [provided] in Christ Jesus,"* [10]

This means (as explained in Romans 4:16) that salvation is for anyone who freely chooses to repent and accept Christ as their Saviour. Let me make this absolutely clear: I believe that there is no limit to the power and effectiveness of Christ's atonement but I also believe that not all individuals will place their faith in that atonement. All fell in Adam, now anyone can be redeemed in Christ, provided they repent of their sins and believe that Christ died for them on the cross. Romans 5:2 promises access to the grace of God our Father, if we trust in Christ's atonement.

As well as, and because of, the free gift of salvation and many other unmerited favours, grace brings great joy and hope. Later in Romans 5, in verse 17, we are told that the Christian can *"reign in life"* because of this grace. What wonderful news this is! How many of us suffer from a view of ourselves as victims when the Bible teaches us that – because of God's grace – we are more than conquerors?

Above all, grace offers us a deep insight into the nature of God, who has always taken the initiative by loving faithless mankind. I have focused quite a bit on why we should approach God for salvation and transformation but it is worth asking, in all humility, why should God accept us? The answer can only be, "Because of His grace". In such a God we can put our trust:

> *"He who did not withhold or spare [even] His own*
> *Son but gave Him up for us all, will He not also*
> *with Him freely and graciously give us all [other]*
> *things?"* [11]

If you have truly received Christ because of God's grace, remember that it is only by grace that you will effectively live your Christian life[12].

One of the most beautiful illustrations of God's grace in the Old Testament is the remarkable story of Hosea, the prophet. In Chapter 1 of Hosea (whose name can mean "saviour") God speaks to the prophet:

> " *'Go, take for yourself a wife of whoredom and*
> *have children of whoredom, for the land commits*
> *great whoredom by forsaking the Lord' "* [13]

So, Hosea is to act out an enormously costly prophecy to illustrate God's grace and deferred judgement. He, the *saviour*, son of Beeri (*illustrious, well* or *fountain*) is to marry Gomer (*failure*), a cult prostitute, who is the daughter of Diblaim (*little cakes* – possibly a reference to a kind of occult "communion"). How strikingly similar this is to the story of Christ, sent into this world of darkness and sin to forgive us because of grace and then betroth Himself to an undeserving church! Despite Gomer (Israel) being completely unfaithful God speaks in extraordinarily tender language of His love for her (Chapter 11:1-4). He goes on to ask:

> " 'How can I give you up, Ephraim? How can I
> hand you over, O Israel?. My heart recoils within
> me; my compassion grows warm and tender' " [14]

Hosea then goes on to speak of a work of repentance and a return to God by people who ought to have acknowledged Him all along. Truly:

> "...the goodness of God leadeth thee to
> repentance." [15]

Conviction of Sin

For each individual the first, essential, step towards our own godly improvement is our personal recognition of the need for change. A comparison which I often use is that no one goes to their doctor unless they know or suspect that they have a physical problem. So no one repents before a Holy God until they see their own sinfulness. We have already observed that God considers the human heart to be deceptive above all things, so it is little wonder that we all know people who lead very selfish, destructive lives but who do not seem to see anything wrong with what they are doing. We are experts at justifying our own behaviour and judging everyone else's!

I witnessed a sad example of this a number of years ago. I was evangelising (with a few others) some alcoholics who were homeless in our town. Several of these men lived "up the river"; in other words, they slept on a path beside the river that runs through the town. One of them told me that, in the winter, he would sometimes wake up with his jacket frozen solid to the tarmac path. What a way for man, made in the image of God, to live! How far we have fallen! Let me call this man Bill (all names, other than my own, have been changed throughout this book). His story is particularly tragic. Bill had once owned his own house but was now enslaved to alcohol and – by the first time I met him - he owned nothing.

Horrendously, someone from whom Bill had allegedly stolen money had, after reading the Koran, sawn off one of his hands (which was restored by the skill of surgeons). He had only escaped worse injuries by diving through an upstairs window. Bill's life was utterly ruined by alcohol and by his unwillingness and inability to change.

On the last occasion when I met Bill he had been diagnosed by his doctor to have just six months to live. I and others told him about the love of God, and His ability to transform him (one other alcoholic, delivered by Christ, used to joke that for him Jesus had turned wine into furniture!). But Bill refused to acknowledge his need of any help. He saw nothing wrong with his life and just wanted more money to continue living it the way he had chosen. Bill died shortly afterwards, still denying the God who loved him.

Perhaps no one who reads this story can equal the drama and tragedy of Bill's life and death? However, we all find it very difficult to acknowledge that there could be flaws in our characters, which are perhaps more subtle than Bill's but which are equally heinous in God's eyes. These flaws do not simply "go away" by themselves, nor can we make them go away by our own efforts; they form part of our very nature (the Bible calls this "the flesh"). The Bible also defines such flaws as "iniquity" or "sin" because, to a Holy God, they offer enduring evidence of the Fall and they continue to separate us in areas of our lives, from Him. It is human nature to conceal sin whereas God sees it all and if it remains unconfessed He will expose it, in due time. Furthermore, because of God's justice and our inherent flaws, He must judge sin, unless He forgives it. Do we want to be judged, or forgiven?

God's justice also demands, I believe, some opportunity for us to see and acknowledge our sinfulness (as He sees it). At the end of this age, Jude prophesies that, when Christ returns, recognition of evil will be granted to those who live in darkness:

> *"[The Lord will come] To execute judgement upon all, and to convince all that are ungodly among them of their ungodly deeds…"* [16]

In John's Gospel, Jesus is reported as saying that the work of the Holy Spirit includes this act of revealing and reproving what is false and wicked:

> *"And when He [the Holy Spirit] is come, He will reprove the world of sin, and of righteousness, and of judgement."* [17]

The word *"reprove"* (*elegcho*) is translated *"convince"* in Titus1:9. This word speaks of an illumination of what is wrong and a conviction of what is right. Without this gracious act of enlightenment by God we would never see the difference between sin and righteousness. We could not distinguish spiritual light from darkness. Paul beautifully expresses this work of the Holy Spirit:

> *"But when anything is exposed and reproved by the light, it is made visible and clear; and where everything is visible and clear there is light."* [18]

God shines the light of His truth and righteousness on the individual human heart, exposing what was hidden because of shame or deception.

This conviction of sinfulness comes as a huge shock to human pride. David graphically explained his own conviction of sin in a number of Psalms. For example, in Psalms 88:7 he movingly described the power and effect of conviction:

> *"Your anger lies heavy upon me, and I am crushed beneath its waves."* [19]

Part of this process of the conviction of sin is the absolute realisation of the legitimacy of God's right to judge us. We are guilty as charged. We are like criminals whose guilt has been demonstrably proven and who have no recourse to clemency outside the undeserved mercy of the judge.

Another aspect of conviction, then, lies in the emotional and mental anguish of the acknowledgement of our complete need for mercy – there is nothing of merit within man by which we can make a just appeal to God. Having said that, there may also be a sense of relief and appropriateness when we honestly confront our sinful condition for the first time. Whatever our feelings, there is no place for pride in any of this. That is why some react so angrily when convicted of sin by the Holy Spirit. But many others react by asking God a similar question to that of the Philippian jailer in Acts 16:30, *"What must I do to be saved?"* Or we think of the words of Peter when Jesus performed the miracle of the fish:

> *"When Simon Peter saw what had happened, he fell on his knees before Jesus and said, 'Go away from me, Lord! I am a sinful man!' "* [20]

On the night when God revealed all of this to me for the first time He clearly and graciously demonstrated both His existence and His infinite love for me. I was then shown, very graphically, that the barrier between God and me was my pride. I was literally shown a brick wall with the word "Pride" sprayed, like a graffito, on the wall. God enabled me to understand that He would not work in my life until this barrier came down. I had to come to Him on His terms, not my own! As I acknowledged and repented of this barrier, in the first enlightened prayer I had ever prayed, God graciously led me through the process of redemption, step-by-step. I immediately knew that my sins were forgiven and that I had become a child of God!

Repentance

Without repentance there is never any real or lasting change. It is an essential first step to inner transformation. Repentance is the proper, most honest, human response to the conviction of sin. Having had the light of God's truth and righteous requirements shone into our lives, we can only humble ourselves before a Holy God and respond with a plea of "guilty". How we shrink from taking personal responsibility for our own misdemeanours! How we love to plead "innocent", or claim "it was his fault, not mine" - even in the face of overwhelming evidence to the contrary! Repentance runs counter to human nature, so it must begin with a humble acknowledgement of our own need for forgiveness.

What helps us to understand biblical repentance is to see it as a process rather than as a single event. Firstly, we are convinced of general sinfulness by the Holy Spirit, who often uses the Bible to shine a light into our spirits, minds and hearts. This then produces a realisation and acceptance of specific, personal sin. Secondly, the individual must sincerely say "sorry" to God (and perhaps to other people). Thirdly, the forgiveness that is sought from God must be accepted by faith, rejecting all condemnation. Fourthly, there must be a change of heart and mind, strengthened by God, combined with the individual's determination not to repeat the sin. Fifthly, the individual must be prepared to "walk in the light", that is, to allow the continual scrutiny of the Holy Spirit into her or his life. Finally, restitution (repayment) must be made for any sin committed against a person or people. It is worth noting here that this process appears to be best understood during times of revival when the Holy Spirit, who convicts of sin, is most manifestly at work.

The most common Greek word for repentance is *metanoia*, indicating not merely a sense of regret or sorrow, but rather a change of heart or mind. True repentance is not only an outward expression of sorrow for sin, it also expresses a strong yearning for inner transformation and a determination to co-operate with God to effect that change. It is the firm conviction that, "I cannot – must not - remain as I am".

In Luke's version of the Great Commission, Jesus commands His disciples to preach repentance as a universal requirement. It is to be taught as a condition for forgiveness, therefore for salvation (Luke 24:47). Peter incorporates strong teaching on repentance into his Pentecost Sermon, in Acts 2:38. In Luke 13:3 the eternal significance of repentance is explained by Jesus:

"I tell you, No: but unless you repent – [that is] change your mind for the better and heartily amend your ways with abhorrence of your past sins – you will all likewise perish and be lost [eternally]." [21]

Due to the very serious nature of this, we must "*bring forth fruits befitting repentance*"[22]. In other words, inner change must be real and lasting. It must produce a fundamental transformation of character, thought and behaviour. Repentance includes a turning away from "*dead works*" (human attempts to please God). Do not be overwhelmed by discouragement if change does not prove to be easy or quick. Luke 5:32 tells us that repentance is for sinners (not the righteous) and in 2 Timothy 2:25 we are told that repentance is a gift from a gracious God. We could not *see* sin, *repent* of it, or gain *victory* over it without the gracious help of a loving God! What is equally clear is that no human being has ever lived who has not needed to repent, regularly. The question is, are we prepared to be this honest about ourselves? Repentance is not only an essential step in the conversion experience: for the Christian it forms a critical part of what is referred to as *sanctification* – the on-going process empowered by the Holy Spirit that makes us increasingly righteous. We must, as disciples, cultivate an attitude of on-going openness to the correction of the Holy Spirit as He convicts us of sin. The disciple must also learn to accept God's response to genuine repentance: forgiveness.

Redemption

Redemption is most easily illustrated by comparing it with the practice of borrowing money from a Pawn Shop, against one's possessions. Such shops thrive, in hard economic times, when those who have become needy may – often as a last, desperate resort - trade in treasured possessions for money. These possessions are held in the shop for an agreed period of time but can be "redeemed" (bought back) if the original owner returns with the correct ticket (proof of ownership) along with the agreed price of redemption. This process corresponds with the desire of God to restore

His creation to a state of grace; to redeem a world foolishly "sold" to Satan by Adam, the fickle steward of creation.

In the Old Testament, this economic provision for poverty is expressed, through God's gracious social economics, by creating a clear material parable of the coming Messiah. We see in Leviticus 25:25 and Ruth Chapters 1-4 an explanation and an example of the so-called "*goel*" in operation. The "*goel*" was the kinsman-redeemer, who would redeem the land or person of any impoverished Israelite who had been forced to sell his possessions or to sell himself into slavery to pay his debts. In Ruth's case she put her trust in Boaz (a type of Christ) who was willing to redeem Ruth after her nearest relative (perhaps representing the Law) found the price too high to pay and who gave way to grace. In Numbers 35:12-14 and Deuteronomy 19:1-3 the *goel* can also be an avenger of innocent blood, thus indicating that salvation and judgement both ultimately belong to our Redeemer, Christ. All of this gives us a wonderful picture of the Incarnate Saviour, Jesus Christ. Even before the Law was given God showed His willingness to redeem His people (Exodus 6:6 expresses God's desire to redeem the Children of Israel from slavery in Egypt).

In Job 19:25 we are given an even more explicit Old Testament reference to the Messiah. Job puts his trust in his personal Redeemer:

> *"For I know that my Redeemer and Vindicator*
> *lives, and at last – the Last One – He will stand*
> *upon the Earth;"* [23]

Job predicts that a Redeemer, already alive in his day, "will" (future tense) stand upon this Earth as his personal Redeemer. This is a remarkable and very early revelation of Christ and of Job's personal need for grace.

In Romans 8:3 Paul was inspired to express this idea of redemption powerfully and beautifully:

> *"For God has done what the Law could not do,*
> *[its power]being weakened by the flesh [that is, the*
> *entire nature of man without the Holy Spirit].*

*Sending His own Son in the guise of sinful flesh
and as an offering for sin, [God] condemned sin
in the flesh — subdued, overcame, deprived it of its
power [over all who accept that sacrifice]."* [24]

Adam had "sold" his relationship with God, along with his innocence and that of his descendants, having been deceived because of his weakness and by the serpent's cunning. Now a second "Adam" (Christ) had come in human form to pay the price to redeem mankind back to God. A mankind which was now under the power of Satan. Redemption reminds us of the cost that God, in Christ, had to pay to "buy" us back to Himself. A very high price had to be paid for human sin: the Righteous Judge could not simply ignore it:

*"…though He was [so very] rich, yet for your sakes
He became [so very] poor, in order that by His
poverty you might become enriched — abundantly
supplied."* [25]

This is a wonderful description of Christ's willingness to pay the price to redeem mankind. He willingly agreed to pay this awful price even before man was created. He agreed to leave heaven and take on human flesh, to suffer on the cross, to buy us back. Because of Jesus those who believe in Him are no longer slaves to sin; we are free and forgiven in Christ. Furthermore, this purchase has provided everything that we need to live godly lives as a result of this freedom.

There are many important theological terms for what Christ achieved on the cross but, at a personal level, it is sufficient for you to believe that, "Christ died for me!" Having believed that and experienced God's redemption, you can then go on to appreciate this wonderful atonement more fully.

New Birth

All the good things that died in Adam, including his innocence and his eternal spiritual relationship with God, can be restored through Christ because of the work of redemption. New birth is an individual, inner, spiritual transformation wrought because of salvation. The atonement (Christ's death on the cross for the sins of humanity) - when believed and received by the individual - brings forgiveness, the abolition of the righteous penalty of the Law and the gift of the imputed righteousness of Christ. Furthermore, it brings, because of God's wonderful grace, the "right" to become a child of God. New birth means, for the believer, that the deadened spirit within us comes to life and our former alienation from God is replaced by the spirit of adoption so that we can cry out to our God, *"Abba, Father"*[26].

Whilst religious practice concentrates upon external appearances and rituals, the New Covenant speaks principally of the restoration of our personal relationship with God (who is Spirit) through the spiritual, inner transformation of the individual, in Christ. For Christians, new birth also results in a new, covenant relationship with God, whereby the promises of God in the New Testament are now all potentially made accessible through Christ.

This Father-son relationship began with the creation of man, who was made in the image and likeness of God from the dust of the ground (Genesis 2:7) and was breathed into by God to give him life. In a very real sense God was Adam's "Father". And in that same creative sense God is the Father of every human being. But just as in a natural father-son relationship a son may be disinherited and separated from his father because of his behaviour, this Father-son relationship between God and mankind ended with Adam's sin and his banishment from the presence of God.

In the New Testament we see the full significance of individual regeneration, made possible by Christ's sacrifice:

> *"But as many as received Him, to them gave He power to become the sons of God, even to them that believe on His name; which were born, not of blood, nor of the will of the flesh, nor of the will of man, but of God."* [27]

Here we see clearly that new birth gives us a new Father, a new family and a new inheritance! We are also transformed within: God brings life to our deadened spirits and we are now enabled to commune with Him. When Jesus taught His disciples to pray, in Matthew 6:9, He gave them an extraordinarily intimate manner of addressing Almighty God, as *"Our Father"*. This is only made possible when we become new creations in Christ[28].

So if we are born again through an act of Holy Spirit regeneration, and God is our Father, does this new birth not indicate a complete doing away with the old nature and life, together with an embracing of God's nature and His pathway of transforming truth?

> *"Whereby are given unto us exceeding great and precious promises: that by these ye might be partakers of the divine nature, having escaped the corruption that is in the world through lust."* [29]

The latter part of the verse is a reference to the Fall in Eden. So God - doing what man and the Law could not do, by His awesome grace - has bought back those who believe in and accept personally the sacrifice of Christ. As a result, He has given us new birth, into His own family and – without removing free will from us – has begun to transform our inner man so that we will choose to live to please Him who gave everything for us. This is Good News!

The New Testament teaching on new birth is clearly expressed in the third chapter of John's Gospel. Jesus responds to a very honest, quizzical statement by Nicodemus, a Pharisee brought up under the Law. In verse 2 Nicodemus acknowledges the divine inspiration for Jesus' teaching. He then receives a response that he had not bargained for! Jesus tells him that:

> *"…unless a person is born again (anew, from above), he cannot ever see – know, be acquainted with [and experience] – the kingdom of God."* [30]

In order to enter and experience a spiritual kingdom we must first experience spiritual re-birth. Nicodemus, unsurprisingly, was puzzled – how can we re-enter our mother's womb (his thinking was entirely of this physical world)? Jesus repeated the command before going on to explain new birth:

> *"The wind blows (breathes) where it will; and though you hear its sound, yet you neither know where it comes from nor where it goes. So it is with everyone who is born of the Spirit."* [31]

Another very clear explanation of this process is contained in the Letter to the Romans. In the first three chapters of Romans the need for salvation is clearly established, then God's way of salvation is laid out in Romans Chapter 4.

Chapters 5-8 then speak of a dramatic result of this salvation (discussed briefly below): our new life in Christ. Any new life has to begin with a new birth, giving rise to a profound sense of a new identity and destiny. After our sins are forgiven, as a result of faith in Christ's awesome sacrifice on the cross, the Holy Spirit regenerates our own (dead) spirit, so that we enter into eternal life and – from that moment onwards – we are enabled to have fellowship (even kinship) with God Himself.

Newness of Life

A new birth logically leads to a new life. The Bible has much to say about this new life in Christ, including the transformational nature of its power within the faithful and persevering disciple. This new power and life are provided by the indwelling Holy Spirit because of the disciple's new position *in Christ*. Power and life are two of the benefits of the New Covenant made between God and man. This Covenant is sure because it has been sealed with the blood of Christ.

The verse quoted above, 2 Peter 1:4, promises that as a result of God's precious promises we can be partakers of His divine nature. The word "*partakers*" (*koinonos*) means those who share in, become partners with, and fellowship closely with. The word "*nature*" (*phusis*) means here disposition or character. These words give us much cause for rejoicing! We can share, in Christ (through the work of the Holy Spirit), all that God has and is. We can also take on something of His character through a process of transformation, so that our own characters become more and more godly. This happens as we surrender to His great work within us by trusting in His promises. We will never become "gods", as the serpent promised Eve, but we can become so spiritually engrafted into God as to take on something of His nature (His character and disposition). So the new birth and new life are not a mere patching up of the old life – they are much more radical than that! The new life that we can have in Christ is completely different from our old lives, to which we must now consider ourselves dead.

One of the clearest biblical explanations of our transition from the old path of sin, through new birth and into newness of life, is found in Romans 6:3-4. Here, Paul explains this initiation into a new life:

> "*Know ye not, that so many of us who were baptized into Jesus Christ were baptized into His death? Therefore we are buried with Him by baptism into death: that like as Christ was raised up from the dead by the glory of the Father, even so we also should walk in newness of life.*" [32]

By fully identifying with Christ in baptism we share in His death and resurrection. If we are in Christ we *shall* be raised from the dead but *now* we enter into a new spiritual life, from spiritual death. The phrase "*should walk in newness of life*" implies the necessary co-operation of the disciple in this process. It is not my belief that God forces anyone to follow Him.

Romans also specifically makes it clear that this new life is characterised – among other benefits - by freedom from slavery to sin. Sin is no longer a compulsive, irresistible force in our natures if we have truly experienced the new birth. The Christian is now a "slave of righteousness" whereas his old life was characterised, at its best, by vain attempts to "be good". In Romans 7:6 Paul goes on to say:

> *"But now we are delivered from the law [of Moses],*
> *that being dead wherein we were held; that we*
> *should serve in newness of spirit, and not in the*
> *oldness of the letter."* [33]

Our new lives are spiritual, but they also have benefits for the soul and body, making available to the disciple constant energy, strength, wisdom and everything else that is needed (this is not to say that Christians cannot fall sick or grow weary!). In Romans 8:1-13 Paul celebrates our forgiveness in Christ and then speaks of our on-going obligation to walk in the spirit: not the flesh. We still have daily choices to make:

> *"For if ye live after the flesh, ye shall die: but if ye,*
> *through the Spirit do mortify the deeds of the body,*
> *ye shall live."* [34]

The equation is simple: if you live to please the flesh you die. If you live to please the Spirit you live.

This, of course, indicates that salvation is a process, not merely a single event. This process must begin with the new birth (salvation or conversion are terms that are sometimes used as synonyms for new birth but they mean different things). Salvation proceeds from the point of conversion towards an ever-increasing maturity (or "perfection"). We are not just saved from the *penalty* of sin. Whoever is in Christ is being saved from the *power* of sin and one day the Christian will be saved from the *presence* of sin. Before the foundation of the world Christ was slain for you but salvation begins, as your individual experience, with your new birth, which leads to a lifetime of outworking and growing into the new spiritual man or woman whom God has designed you to be. One aspect of this is encouragingly expressed in 1 John 1:7:

"But if we walk in the light, as He is in the light, we have fellowship one with another, and the blood of Jesus Christ His Son cleanseth us from all sin". [35]

Note that the continuous access to the forgiveness of God, for those who believe in the blood of Christ and repent, causes us to have true fellowship "in the light" with God and with one another. We are never alone in this new life!

Deliverance From Evil

In 1 Peter 1:5-10 salvation through Christ is described using past, present and future tenses. Even before putting our faith in Christ, God protected and shielded us. I myself would have been killed on a number of occasions were it not for the mercy of God. On one such occasion, when I was a student, I rolled down a steep grassy bank only to stop right on the edge of a sea cliff, with my legs dangling in space. What stopped me rolling just once more? It certainly was not gravity! You can probably point to similar mercies in your own life. In addition, by His grace He brought us to that point when we could enter into a salvation already prepared for us in Christ. We were then, at the point of salvation, saved from the penalty of our sin and rescued from the hold that sin had over our lives.

As indicated above, for the Christian, salvation is also a present and continuous process as we continue to be sanctified and transformed, while the residual effects of evil in our bodies and souls are cleaned away. God continues to protect and deliver the Christian on a daily basis as He is an ever-present help in times of trouble. Salvation also awaits the Christian as a future fulfilment of the fullness of God's promises in Christ. It is stored up for us as an inheritance, an aspect of which is eternal life in the presence of God, after we have been removed from the very presence of evil.

In Revelation 22:11 the writer states:

"He that is unjust, let him be unjust still: and he

which is filthy, let him be filthy still: and he that
is righteous, let him be righteous still: and he that
is holy, let him be holy still." [36]

So a point will come when the moral condition of each man will be categorised by God, our holy judge, and each person will remain in that general state permanently.

In Revelation 7:14-17 there is a wonderful picture of the blissful future relationship between those saints removed from the great tribulation and their God:

"And I said unto him, Sir, thou knowest. And He said to me, These are they which came out of the great tribulation, and have washed their robes, and made them white in the blood of the Lamb. Therefore are they before the throne of God, and serve Him day and night in His temple: and He that sitteth on the throne shall dwell among them. They shall hunger no more, neither thirst any more; neither shall the sun light on them. Nor any heat. For the Lamb which is in the midst of the throne shall feed them, and shall lead them unto living fountains of waters: and God shall wipe away all tears from their eyes." [37]

I make no apology for such a lengthy quotation, as this passage wonderfully describes the intimacy, protection, provision and worship that will be the inheritance of these formerly suffering saints. Note that those referred to above *"have washed their robes"*. Clearly they will not be passive in receiving the righteousness obtained because of *"the blood of the Lamb"*. We have a responsibility to avail ourselves of God's means for making us holy and acceptable to Him.

The Book of Revelation also makes the fate of Satan, the author of evil and sin, very clear. When he is bound up for ever in his eternal prison – along with his malevolent army of followers – the presence of evil will have been removed from mankind. The serpent will no longer be able to deceive and corrupt. Those who are in Christ will remain in the presence of God, their Father, for an eternity without tears, suffering or evil of any kind.

CHAPTER 3

BINDING UP THE BROKEN HEART AND DEVELOPING A HEART THAT IS PLEASING TO GOD

Emotional Healing and Wholeness

For the Christian disciple God is no longer distant or remote. Over and over again in the New Testament we are told that Christ dwells in our hearts by faith and that the Holy Spirit indwells our newly regenerate spirits. As well as existing universally, God also chooses to live within the individual Christian. The Galatians knew what it was to begin to have Christ formed[1] within them but they allowed legalism to interrupt this process, so that Paul had to pray for it to begin again.

Because God indwells the Christian, He can directly influence the human soul via the spirit. When we accept Christ as our Saviour we do not merely receive a "patched-up" soul: mind, emotions, will and character. The new birth and the indwelling Holy Spirit mean that, as we live moment by moment in the Spirit, we can continuously manifest His qualities and values. By co-operating with the Holy Spirit our motivations, thoughts and feelings are changed. However, God will not "take us over", we must come to His grace in a constant attitude of faith and submission. As we do so we experience as well as function in His inspiration. Increasingly, we love with His unlimited love, rather than our own finite emotions.

As our hearts are purified and healed they become increasingly open to His influence. Take courage! We tend to focus on those things that still need to be changed but we should also thank God daily for the work already accomplished in us. For the true disciple bearing good fruit is spiritually natural.

When I first became a Christian I found that one of the areas which God began to focus on with His sanctifying and healing power was the area of my heart, my emotional being. As a child I had a very secure but mobile home life. Because of my father's job I changed schools and friendships frequently. Perhaps as a result I became a shy, introverted and extremely sensitive boy. For example, I refused to eat in other people's houses. By my late teens I had immersed myself in literature and I had become an imaginative and thoughtful but very intense and insecure young man, who eventually drank heavily to ease my emotional dislocation. I brought some of this insecurity – which had manifested itself in increasingly extreme and sudden mood swings – into my Christian life and into my marriage. My inexplicable frustrations and unfounded discouragements were fed by a deep-seated self-centredness that had yet fully to surrender to my new life in Christ. But God (I love those two words), but God loved me despite my emotional mess and He applied the sword of His truth to the Gordian Knot (a knot famous in antiquity for seeming impossible to untie) of my hopelessly entangled, negative emotions. And He applied the oil of His Spirit to the wounds and disappointments in my heart. However, because of the negative and uncertain experiences of the volatility of my own emotions, I struggled as a young Christian with the question of whether God could use this heart of mine for any useful thing. Or did "dying to self" imply a death to all emotions, as well as to sinful desires? Once again, a study of the Bible helped me to answer this question.

The more I searched Scriptures, the more I saw the importance to God of the transformed human heart. In several passages, such as Psalms 147:3, God promises to heal the heart. How does He do this? By adopting us as His children, God becomes our loving, merciful and wise Father. Not all children have happy memories of what the word "father" means to them so this new, intimate relationship with God begins a healing and restorative process in our souls. Being in Christ also brings purification, as the sinful, conflicting tendencies of the heart are overcome and in their place we begin to develop the positive fruits of the Spirit (such as peace, joy and love). And the operation of the Holy Spirit in our hearts brings emotional healing. One of the pictures of the Spirit in the Bible is of an aromatic, healing oil. This oil, when the heart is open to Him, can go deeper than the damage inflicted by the worst emotional wound, bringing cleansing and healing.

I remember praying with George years ago. He had been devastated by a failed relationship, to the point where he could not think or speak with any clarity. He lived in a cloud of confusion. As I prayed with him I had a picture of God removing a boulder from a stream. The boulder was George's grief and pain, blocking the flow of healthy thoughts and feelings – as well as of the Spirit – in his life. I told him what I believed God was going to do and encouraged him to open up to the ministry of the Holy Spirit. After two weeks of tears, laughter and release George was able to converse and even preach fluently. His self-esteem was restored in Christ and he subsequently married a fine Christian lady. I was able to observe the permanent and radical changes in his life. God wants to heal our wounds and take the "boulders" out of our hearts!

Elizabeth had been cheated out of an inheritance, by relatives whom she had trusted. She was wounded and embittered by the experience, so much so that when she talked about it many years later it was as if the betrayal had occurred the day before. Unhealed emotional pain festers in our hearts and shapes our characters in negative ways. Bitterness makes us angry, suspicious and critical. As she allowed God to minister to her heart, Elizabeth was changed into a compassionate, understanding and deeply prayerful lady. She had found riches in Christ far superior to the material wealth she had lost.

Both Elizabeth and George had been so deeply wounded in life that their hearts had become wellsprings of trouble and death, rather than blessing and life. When God bound up their broken hearts, healing unseen wounds, He transformed their characters and made them whole in Him.

The Bible teaches us, in Romans 10:10, that it is with the heart that we believe, so purifying and healing the heart to make it more receptive to faith is important to God and to the Christian disciple. God has also promised to write His laws in the Christian mind and heart (Hebrews 8:10), so He must heal and purify the heart in order to make it more receptive to His commandments.

One way to purify the heart is to humble it with fasting. In Psalms 35:13 the writer says, *"I humbled my soul with fasting"*[2]; there are occasions when the carnal demands of the soul and body need to be disciplined, when a special time is set aside to focus every part of us on the Lord. I would link this with the command of Mark 12:33:

> *"... love God with all your heart and with all your*
> *mind and with all your strength..."* [3]

This verse clearly indicates that the worship of God involves your whole being. Hunger and thirst for God can grip a soul influenced by the Holy Spirit[4] and the soul can be redeemed[5]. In 3 John 2 the apostle greets Gaius by communicating a prayer for his general health and specifically for the health of his soul (translated "spirit" in the GNB):

> *"Beloved, I pray that all may go well with you and*
> *that you may be in good health, just as it is well*
> *with your soul."* [6]

These biblical insights coincide with my observation that modern therapists are increasingly exploring the links between mental, emotional and physical health – and some even recognise the importance of spiritual health. The term "holistic" can be misused but at its best it expresses the need for the whole person to be healthy or to be healed and it acknowledges that each "part" of us affects every other part.

As stated before, my definition of the human soul is inspired by 1 Thessalonians 5:23, which defines our "whole being" as "spirit, soul and body". In turn, the human soul can be defined as being a combination of the will, the mind and the emotions, those parts of us that interact with, and try to make sense of, the world around us. The soul can be transformed by Christ from a state of darkened sinfulness to a state of enlightened grace. The Old Testament in particular, sometimes uses the word "soul" to mean "person" or "spirit" but the sense in which I use the word here is outlined above. If God is interested in transforming us wholly then transformation of the soul is surely an essential part of the divine plan?

The process of the transformation of the soul involves many important steps, including our repentance from sins or negative habits and our acknowledgement of the need for change. The past of each individual, and its lingering effect on the soul, will need to be dealt with; and wholeness will include the need for all aspects of the soul to be set free or healed by the power of God. For this work to take place there is the need for on-going submission of the will to God and His word. Finally, that which is *negative* in the soul (like anxiety) must be replaced by something *positive* (like trust).

God promises, in Isaiah 61, to *"bind up the broken-hearted"* and to heal those in emotional pain:

> *"The Sovereign Lord has filled me with his Spirit. He has chosen me and sent me to bring good news to the poor, to heal the broken-hearted, to announce release to captives and redeem those in prison. He has sent me to proclaim that the time has come when the Lord will save his people and defeat their enemies. He has sent me to comfort all who mourn."* [7]

Jesus quoted this Jubilee proclamation from Isaiah as His manifesto, at the beginning of His public ministry, in Luke 4:16-30. This passage clearly indicates the redemptive and comprehensive nature of the

Messiah's work. By quoting from the Jubilee promises of the Old Testament Jesus defined the goals of His earthly ministry. Indeed, He states that the fulfilment of the Jubilee promises of God have now been ushered in through Him. This Jubilee proclamation forms the basis of the New Covenant – a set of promises with conditions made by God to each believer. The Jubilee proclamation includes promises of healing and help for the human soul.

We see this in the early reference to *"good news to the poor"*. These are the poor in spirit or heart (not the financially poor). Such people are far more receptive to God's offer of help than those who believe themselves to be "rich". Then we have the wonderful promise to *"bind up the broken-hearted"*. The Hebrew verb for *"bind up"* has various aspects of meaning, including: "healing", "wrapping up", "girding about" and "stopping". So Jesus clearly saw His redemptive work as a holistic ministry, which would result in forgiveness of sin and also the ministry of "healing" the human heart, "strengthening" it and "stopping" its hopeless suffering. This passage in Isaiah goes on to promise the believer a spirit of praise and joy instead of a spirit of heaviness, along with other promises related to the soul of man. In other words, the benefits of Christ's atonement are not limited to the judicial – the forgiveness of sins – His atoning work also makes available to those who believe in Him a process of healing and sanctification of the soul.

Before he is born again, an individual's soul is held captive to sin. It is driven by its Fallen Nature into constant thoughts and feelings of selfishness. Emotions, for those who – according to Paul – are *"slaves to sin"*[8] can only be experiences and expressions of the pain and bondage of this slavery to sinful passions. Psychiatrists observe that man is driven by deep-seated passions. The Bible came to this conclusion long before modern psychiatry. In Ephesians 2:3, Paul describes the history of his and their souls, before conversion to Christ:

> *"Amongst whom also we all once conducted ourselves in the lusts of our flesh, fulfilling the desires of the flesh and of the mind."*[9]

Indeed, it can be argued that these sinful passions are the perverted echoes of the pure motivations within Adam's soul, created by God in him and expressed positively in his state of innocence in the Garden of Eden. For example, Adam took delight in his intimacy with God: since the Fall this positive desire has been twisted into a constantly unfulfilled human search for significance, identity and meaning. Adam also worshipped the one, true, God: fallen man is capable of worshipping anyone or anything else. Adam was instructed to love Eve and to procreate: fallen man has debased this desire into insatiable and often dark sexual urges. Adam exercised delegated authority: fallen man craves control and power. Adam was a good steward of the Earth: fallen man exploits it.

Satisfaction of these dominant, demanding passions within fallen man can provide temporary feelings of joy and pleasure. But the slave to sin more often experiences the lash than the approval of his master. Unredeemed man is portrayed in the Bible as being tormented by negative – often irrational – feelings of fear, guilt, anxiety and a host of other destructive feelings. It is for this reason, amongst others, that human emotions of any kind have frequently been characterised by Christians as nothing more than a set of irrational and unreliable experiences which are to be avoided or pacified.

Even in Charismatic or Pentecostal circles with their emphasis on powerful, personal encounters with God the term "soulish" is often used as a criticism to dismiss any activity or experience that is considered to be merely emotional, having no spiritual substance or value. How, then, could God have any use for human emotions? Surely they are so intrinsically unstable and unreliable as to be of no benefit to God or to any genuine disciple? The Christian, indeed, must take care not to judge or weigh the value of things merely by how they make her or him feel. What is good for us does not always *feel* good: and what feels good is not necessarily morally or spiritually good. The Christian must beware using only his or her emotions as a measure for spiritual experiences. On the other hand, we all need to take seriously those genuine Christian testimonies that include references to transformed feelings, as a result of the work of the Holy Spirit within the receptive human heart.

If it were the case that God has no place in His plan for human emotions at all, then there would be no positive mention of the soul and its emotions in the Bible. God Himself is referred to as having and experiencing pure and holy feelings, according to Scriptures. Of course, there is all the difference in the world between carnal feelings (deriving from the Fallen Nature) and feelings expressed by the same words but which are attributes of the Divine Nature, or which are inspired in the human spirit and soul by the Holy Spirit. For example, if we take the word "love", we know that it can be used to mean anything from having a strong liking for something ("I love ice cream") to obsessive, romantic love for another human being. However, God's kind of love is completely unselfish – it is not about the satisfaction of a personal need. God's love took Christ to the cross. It is a love that always considers the other before self. This is very different from love as we understand it in this world! Nevertheless, it is expressed emotionally as well as sacrificially by Christ, moving Him on one occasion to weep over Jerusalem.

To help us to understand this, let us briefly consider the "fruit of the Spirit":

> *"But the fruit of the Spirit is love, joy, peace, longsuffering, kindness, goodness, faithfulness, gentleness, self-control. Against such there is no law. And those who are in Christ have crucified the flesh with its passions and desires. If we live in the Spirit, let us also walk in the Spirit."* [10]

Most of the words in this wonderful list of qualities have resonances in everyday experiences. For example, we feel joy when our team wins, or when we earn a promotion, or for many other reasons. But there are significant differences between these feelings of joy and the spiritual joy described by Paul. Firstly, everyday joy is temporary whereas spiritual joy endures eternally – no matter what is happening to us or around us. Secondly, everyday joy is the result of self-gratification – of something going right for us – whereas spiritual joy comes from knowing God's constancy in love and grace. Thirdly, everyday joy has its origin in the material world around us, whilst spiritual joy springs from the Spirit's impulse. So "spiritual" joy is not the same as "earthly" or "everyday" joy: it has a different source and it feels different – more pure and significant.

Some of the words in the list in Galatians, quoted above, are sadly lacking in most people's experiences. For example, take the word "peace". Jesus is called the "Prince of Peace" in Isaiah 9:6. True peace originates from Him and is only experienced when we are in relationship with Him. Paul says, in Philippians 4:6, that the Christian is to be *anxious for nothing*. This sounds impossible! In the next verse he goes on to say that you and I are to let the peace of God *"guard your hearts and minds"*. For the Christian, peace is a gift, it is an arbiter between good and evil, it is a fruit that grows out of a trusting and intimate relationship with the Prince of Peace. The person who does not know Christ cannot know this peace. And the Christian who takes his mind and heart off Christ will quickly lose this peace.

When we let God do His wonderful work in our hearts, our feelings, as well as our motivations, are purified and transformed. Past hurts are healed and our emotional and moral "baggage" is surrendered to God. All this legacy from our past has already been dealt with on the cross and – because of His grace – we are set free to be, do and feel as He intended. This all requires the aid of the Holy Spirit. Remember, you cannot change yourself: it is the grace of God that enables us to change.

A good example of the change God wants to make in us is implied in the repeated command that we are to "love our neighbours as ourselves". It could be argued that we tend to love ourselves too much and others far too little! However, it is my observation that many people do not love themselves at all, so how can they love their neighbour? They have never experienced unselfish love, so how can they know what it feels like, or how to recognise or communicate it?

I remember when God powerfully revealed His love for me. As a young Christian on one occasion I experienced considerable disillusionment and rejection when helping to plant a church. At that time – it was the summer – I had my morning prayers in our garden. After a particularly difficult week I sought God for a solution to my dilemma. What could I do to fix the problem? I felt God answer me very simply but powerfully, "Brian, I love you." To my shame I said something like, "I know that, Lord, but what I really need is a solution to this situation." My entire focus was on what I understood to be the problem and on how to fix it. Actually, I was not focused on the real problem, which was that I did not really *know* the extent of His love! Each morning, as I sought for the answer to my problem, I felt God repeat the same words to me, gently but insistently. At last, after several mornings, I finally got it! God's love was the answer to all of my problems! This was a profound revelation to me and has remained with me during the decades since. This need for a personal revelation of God's love is why Paul prays for the Ephesian church:

> *"That He may grant you...to be strengthened with might through His spirit in the inner man...to comprehend with all the saints what is the width and length and depth and height – to know the love of Christ..."* [11]

Love has to be *known*, it has to be experienced in our innermost beings for us to understand divine love properly. God's love can only be experienced, known, with the help of the Holy Spirit. This love comes by revelation, it is received by the individual's spirit and then floods the mind and heart. It then motivates us to love our neighbours as we now know that we are loved. We need the power of the Holy Spirit in our feeble souls to receive this revelation. The passage quoted above goes on to speak of the Christian being *"rooted and grounded"* in the love of God. This divine love, flowing through our very beings, produces the fruit of love, which can then edify and bless others. He (Paul) speaks at the end of this chapter of the Christian being filled with *"the fullness of God"*. This does not mean that we are filled with God's divinity but rather it means that we are filled with His love.

Divine love, the "better way" of 1 Corinthians 13, should motivate the Christian in all that he or she thinks, feels and does. Is there someone you cannot love, no matter how hard you try? Perhaps they have treated you badly, or spoken ill of you? Christ died for that person and He loves them (though not necessarily what they do!). Let God love that person through you, having forgiven them and repented of all wrong feelings. Pray out of God's love for them. You cannot pray for someone for long without experiencing God's love for them. Prayer is where we begin to let God love others through us. Bring your mind and heart into harmony with God's mind and heart. This is very challenging but if you wish to obey God and become like Him then you will surrender to this process. The more often you do this, the more your character will be shaped into His likeness and the less you will be haunted by negative thoughts and feelings.

If you wish to become more like Christ then you must – with the aid of the Holy Spirit – think, feel and act more like Him. As you surrender to the work of the Holy Spirit in your "inner man" and do not give up at the first (or the seventy-seventh!) setback, then He will help you by transforming your heart to become more like His. To experience God's love for you is wonderful and is truly life-changing. To experience it for someone else is evidence that you are being transformed into the likeness of Christ.

The Bible promises, indeed commands, many benefits for the Christian mind and heart (including peace, joy, the healing of grief and so on). We can know emotional and mental peace and joy despite challenging circumstances, if we allow God to do His gracious work within us. Indeed, Paul characterises the Kingdom of God as:

> *"For God's Kingdom is not a matter of eating and*
> *drinking, but of the righteousness, peace and joy*
> *which the Holy Spirit gives."* [12]

Remember our earlier point, that God transforms our behaviour and emotions by changing us from "the inside out" – not the other way round. Our external behaviour will never consistently change until we allow God to change our hearts, our motives, our souls. As a consequence of profound inner change, as our behaviour changes, so our characters change and people take note that the Good News "works".

A passage that offers insight into this is 2 Peter 1:4-11. This passage begins with the key promise that we are able to overcome external, worldly temptations, and internal lusts because of the *"divine power"* (verse 3) He has given to believers. This verse also contains an aspiration as well as a description of a current spiritual fact – that we already share in the *"divine nature"*. As a result, Peter goes on to say, we should add *"goodness"* to our *"faith"*. Note that, for the Christian, everything begins with faith. In this case, we embrace the belief that we can live more godly lives than we do now, despite our periodic lapses. Everyone has these lapses – let us not allow them to condemn us out of receiving God's promises, or His wonderful goal for our lives.

To *"goodness"* we should add *"knowledge"*, meaning that goodness leads to a desire to know God better, and that knowledge, in turn, inspires us to even greater goodness as we grow in our knowledge of and intimacy with Him. To these qualities we are to add *"self-control"*: it is vital to appreciate that we have a large part to play in this transformational work within our characters. To self-control we are to add *"endurance"* – this process of improvement takes time, and it can be very costly. Endurance leads to *"godliness"* – note that, by now, real and permanent changes have taken place in our characters; we are genuinely better than we were!

To these, finally, we are to add *"Christian affection"* and *"love"* – so that our characters become full of compassion and unselfishness. If only everyone in the world were like this! If only everyone in the church were like this! If only you or I were more consistently like this! We can be, in Christ.

We can see then, by any honest reading of Scripture, that God has promised to forgive, cleanse, heal and transform our souls, including our hearts and our emotions. This transformation can be real and permanent and it will enable us to walk in *"newness of life"* motivated in thought, feeling and action by hearts filled with faith and integrity. I have personally observed the amazing transformation of many individuals, including George and Elizabeth, who originally put their trust in the wisdom of this world, only to find that "the foolishness of God" (the Gospel), works! There is nothing more wonderful than to observe our gracious God taking away the *"ashes"* of someone's life and replacing them with *"beauty"*. By submitting to His healing we find true wholeness, purpose, freedom and purity.

CHAPTER 4

THE CHRISTIAN MIND

A Personal Testimony

Not again! I winced with disappointment, shame and almost physical pain as, yet again, an unwanted thought forced its way into my mind. Thoughts, for example, of cruelty, judgement or envy towards others. Even as a very young Christian I was acutely aware that these thoughts did not belong in a Christian mind but I had heard little teaching about how to deal with them. I not only felt tainted by these thoughts, I felt condemned and discouraged also. The devil seemed to be able to walk at will through an open door into my mind. When these thoughts kept occurring they appeared so ingrained as to be a part of me. I was supposed to be a "new creation" in Christ but someone had forgotten to inform my brain! I knew that I could not grow in Christ without learning how to become an "overcomer" in my own mind. I had to learn how to defeat the Accuser of the Brethren (Satan) when he planted thoughts as temptations in my mind and then accused me of having them. I knew that I did not want them and that they did not belong in someone who was supposed to have "the mind of Christ".

As I prayed, revelation began to come from the Bible and from the Holy Spirit. I saw, in Genesis, that the serpent tempted Eve with words. Whether these were audible or "heard" in the mind, they became part of her thinking, as she accepted them as true. In Eve's mind doubts must have formed into attitudes of cynicism and defiance – leading to rebellion against God. I also read in the Bible that Jesus was led into the wilderness to be tempted by Satan at the beginning of His public ministry[1]. Satan's weapons were enticing words and ideas, which he hoped Christ would accept in his mind as the truth. Jesus' weapon was not His claim to divinity – He used a weapon that is provided for all believers – the Sword of the Spirit, the Word of God.

As I studied the Bible, I began to appreciate that the words we are attacked with come from the source of temptation and that we have some mighty, spiritual weapons with which we can overcome these attacks on our minds. I saw in 2 Corinthians 10:5 that we are to take every thought captive to Christ. We are never commanded to do anything God has not equipped us for, so I began to take authority over unwanted thoughts. I proclaimed that they did not belong in a mind surrendered to Christ; I quoted Scriptures and took authority over them in Jesus' name.

To my delight and reassurance, I began to experience a transformation in my thinking. Some of these unwanted thoughts and ideas had been conceived in my pre-Christian life and had become stubbornly embedded in my personality. But these mental strongholds also had to move, in Jesus' name. As I continued to take authority over my thoughts, my mind began to clear and much greater peace came into my soul. As my discernment grew[2] I began to sense the enemy's activity even before a thought or image formed in my conscious mind.

This personal process of renewal of my mind will not be completed this side of heaven but measurable progress has been made. During a recent trip to Athens God took me on another step in this process of renewal. He spoke to me about a literal application of Philippians 4:6:

> *"Don't worry about anything, but in all your prayers ask God for what you need, always asking Him with a thankful heart."* [3]

I became much more aware of subtly anxious thoughts in my mind. It is possible to worry about almost anything but anxiety is an enemy of peace and faith. Worrying can become a habit. So, instead of being anxious I lifted up every situation to God in prayer, with an attitude of trust and thanksgiving. As I did so faith, joy and peace were all continually renewed. God our Father wants us all to trust Him absolutely, thanking Him for His unfailing promises and character. In this way, the Christian mind can be set free by truth and filled with peace.

The Logos of God

The truth of God has been revealed in and through the *Logos*, Jesus our Saviour and Lord. The word *logos* conveys the sense of a detailed, systematic and reasonable explanation of something otherwise hidden from our understanding. In the sense that it is meant in the first chapter of John's Gospel, Jesus is the means by which God the Father has communicated Himself to mankind. Jesus came into this world not only to save us from our sins, but also to make comprehensible to us a God whose thoughts are far above our own. In this sense there is never any "new" truth: God in all His unsearchable wonder has always existed and He is the truth. However, the individual Christian and the wider Christian Church are on a journey of ever greater enlightenment, seeking to discover more and more about God by the revelation of the Holy Spirit. The writer to the Hebrews, in Chapter 1:1-2 expresses this wonderful aspect of Christ's mission in this way:

> *"In the past, God spoke to our ancestors many times and in many ways through the prophets, but in these days he has spoken to us through his Son. He is the one through whom God created the universe, the one whom God has chosen to possess all things at the end."* [4]

The Bible is a completed record of the truth of God revealed through

Christ. Without the help of the Holy Spirit, shining His light on God's Word, the human mind would be incapable of any awareness or understanding of the truth about God. Do you remember trying to read the Bible before you became a Christian? I do, and it made little sense to me! As we become increasingly open to the truth of God entering our lives, our minds are renewed and we hold more of that truth with utter conviction. Nevertheless, our knowledge and understanding are necessarily incomplete: we only ever "know in part" this side of eternity.

Another significant issue is relevant here. We will see in the next chapter that many of the attacks levelled against Christians and Christianity come in the form of words, ideas and belief systems – all of which are calculated to rob Christians of their faith by sowing seeds of doubt where there should be assurance. What is God's stated ambition for our minds, in the light of all of this?

Christians often express one of two extreme views concerning the Christian mind. One view expresses an over-confidence in the ability of the educated mind. This view holds that by improving our minds through learning and by the use of rational analysis we can understand God – that understanding is all, and that rational or logical thinking, informed by our five senses, will answer all of our most complicated theological questions. The other extreme opinion views the mind with great suspicion: it sees the mind as being a bit like the human appendix – we're not quite sure what it is for, occasionally it grumbles and we would probably all be better off without it! Sometimes the expression of one of these extreme views is a reaction to the other.

Hearing these opinions preached very forcibly in sermons, over the years, drove me back to the Bible to look for answers. I was astonished to discover just how much it has to say about God's plans and uses for any human mind that is fully surrendered to Him. I also discovered that not all of the statements I was hearing in sermons were accurate reflections of what the Bible actually teaches – they were often clichés that preachers had heard from other preachers. Actually, I was soon left to marvel at the fullness of God's plans for the redemption and renewal of almost every part of the human mind (though not all of its contents!) and the uses to which He wishes to put the mind that is set on Him.

Just one of many explanations of how God wishes to transform, then use, our minds can be found in Ephesians 4:17-32. Far from seeing the human mind as being either supreme or irrelevant, Paul outlines the strong connection between our new birth by the grace of God and the importance of the renewed mind, submitted to God, for continued discipleship. In verse 17 Paul says that we should not walk *"in the vanity of the mind"*: rather we should humbly acknowledge God's existence and our need for continuing submission to Him. In verse 18 the three main consequences of unreformed *"vanity of the mind"* are explained: our understanding is darkened; we are alienated from God; and our hearts become *"blind"*. This in turn, in verse 19, leads to a desensitised immorality, uncleanness and greed. In verse 20 Paul states that if we are in Christ we should not be like this; an inner transformation has taken place in our spirits which ought to be outworked in our thoughts, feelings and behaviour. This is as a result of hearing the truth, faithfully taught (v.21). We must respond to the gracious work of God within us by a deliberate and conscious act, *"Put off the old man, with all its ways"*; the old, sinful nature is beyond help, it must be jettisoned in favour of a new life and character in Christ. Having *"put off"* the sinful nature you and I are commanded to be *"renewed in the spirit of your mind"* (v.23). This phrase connects the work of the Holy Spirit, in our own spirits, with the state and condition of our minds. We are then to *"put on the new man"* (part of which is the renewed mind), which is created *"after God"* (like God) in righteousness and true holiness. As a result of inner transformation, we are then enabled to have changed characters and behaviour. In verses 25-32 Paul lists twenty behavioural consequences of the renewal process he has just described. Encourage yourself by reading and praying over this passage.

Whilst considering the work of God in and through the mind of the true disciple of Christ, I will talk further about these complex but exciting issues under several sub-headings: The Human Mind; The Regenerate Mind; Renewing The Mind; Revelation and The Mind; and The Battlefield of The Mind.

The Human Mind

There are seven key Greek words for the human "mind"[5]. These seven words describe the complex and varied aspects of its functions. In addition to these seven words for the mind, there are other Greek words for "minded", "revelation" and no less than fifteen words for "think". We are used to preachers reminding us of the three main Greek words for "love" but fifteen words for "think"! Clearly, any serious study of the Bible will reveal that God has a purpose for the regenerate mind.

God created within man a rich and complex set of mental faculties, which along with his spirit set him apart from the rest of creation. In the beginning, God created Adam as a living soul. Part of his *living soul* was the gift of an outstanding mind, capable of performing various useful and creative mental functions. In the Garden of Eden these mental abilities operated in the context of an open relationship with God, in a state of innocence, and also as an essential tool for effective stewardship of creation. But the human mind became at once a source of pride, in Adam and Eve, and it provided the opportunity by which Satan could tempt them.

After the Fall every aspect of the human mind immediately degenerated to a profound level of bondage and blasphemy because man had acquired the *"knowledge of good and evil"*. The result of this is that the unregenerate man cannot know God, neither can he have absolutely pure motives, to do the good he would wish to do:

> *"…so then, with my mind I am a slave to the law of God, but with my flesh I am a slave to the law of sin.."* [6]

The *"knowledge of good"* condemns man because it sets a standard too high for him to attain by his own efforts; and the *"knowledge of evil"* opens mankind up to the deceptions discussed in Chapter 5 – as well as opening man up to all manner of sins that begin as mental temptations. The unregenerate man also constantly wavers and is unreliable – he makes promises he can never keep, as Paul says:

*"Was I vacillating when I wanted to do this? Do
I make my plans according to ordinary human
standards, ready to say, 'Yes, yes' and 'No, no' at
the same time?"* [7]

It is my belief that, in Christ, every part of man can be redeemed, if
it is not utterly sinful (such as the "old man", or "the flesh"). As I studied
God's promises for the submitted Christian mind, I noticed how this
complete range of promises covers every key faculty or function of the
mind[8].

The Regenerate Mind

The natural mind of man, since the Fall, is portrayed in the Bible
as being enslaved to base passions, obsessions, selfishness and sin. In
Romans 1:18-32 we see the vicious circle of ever increasing individual
mental and spiritual darkness, leading to increasingly grave behaviour,
which in turn leads to God's judgement.

The Law (of Moses) could not create inner transformation because
it could only expose, not change fallen human nature:

*"but I see in my members another law at war with
the law of my mind, making me captive to the law
of sin that dwells in my members."* [9]

Indeed, the Law has fulfilled its divine purpose:

*"Now before faith came, we were imprisoned
and guarded under the law until faith could be
revealed."* [10]

God's ultimate plan is to transform man so that the Law could be
written, not on stone, but on human hearts and in human minds –
so that it might become a part of human nature, not merely a set of
external observances:

"This is the covenant that I will make with the house of Israel after those days, says the Lord: I will put my laws in their minds, and write them on their hearts, and I will be their God, and they shall be my people." [11]

Most people cherish what they consider to be "freedom of thought" but freedom for the unregenerate mind is merely an illusion based on the knowledge of good and evil and the delusion of what is sown into our minds by the devil. So the unregenerate man operates in a state of moral and mental darkness. The Bible makes it clear that we cannot truly think or act righteously without an inner transformation, wrought by the Holy Spirit and beginning with the new birth. A significant part of the continuing work of the Holy Spirit – in healing, freeing, transforming, sanctifying and enlightening – is done in our minds, via our newly regenerate spirits.

The unregenerate mind is easy prey to the delusions and temptations of the devil but God has several important uses for the regenerate mind. Moreover, the unregenerate mind cannot know God. In 1 Corinthians 1:17–2:16 we see that knowing God is only possible as a result of a revelation delivered by the Holy Spirit, via our own spirits, to the regenerate mind. The things of God, indeed, are "*foolishness*" to anyone who does not know Him:

"For the story and message of the cross is sheer absurdity and folly to those who are perishing and on their way to perdition, but to us who are being saved it is the [manifestation of] the power of God." [12]

God influences the individual "seeker's" mind throughout the process of conviction, repentance, revelation and faith that leads to the new birth. One effect of the new birth is the illumination and sanctification of the mind for the continuing work of grace that will be wrought in it, by the Holy Spirit and by the "*washing of the Word*".

The mind is also - like any faculty, object, skill or instrument that is surrendered to God – potentially useful to God for His own purposes. A good example of God's sanctified use of a human ability or gift is an individual's skill at making music. Such skills existed and were often misused before regeneration but are sanctified and useful to God when fully surrendered, to be used for His glory. When the mind experiences regeneration (new birth) it "comes alive" to an awareness of God. The renewing effect of the new birth on the "inner man" (including the mind) is expressed very clearly in two key Scriptures. In 2 Corinthians 4:16 the word *anakainoo* (to make different, to transform) is translated *"renewed"*:

> *"...Though our outer man is (progressively) decaying and wasting away, yet our inner self is being (progressively) renewed day after day"* [13]

And in Ephesians 4:23 the word *ananeoo* (to make young) is used,

> *"And be constantly renewed in the spirit of your mind – having a fresh mental and spiritual attitude."* [14]

The regenerate mind will focus on that which gives life:

> *"To set the mind on the flesh is death, but to set the mind on the Spirit is life and peace."* [15]

This also requires a disciplined determination, on our part:

> *"Since, therefore, Christ suffered in the flesh, arm yourselves also with the same intention (for whatever has suffered in the flesh has finished with sin)."* [16]

This discipline is not an end in itself, our hope is for something much greater:

*"Therefore prepare your minds for action; discipline
yourselves; set all your hope on the grace that Jesus
Christ will bring to you when He is revealed."* [17]

There are some immediate benefits[18] for our regenerate minds, as we remain in Christ, open to the Holy Spirit and obedient to the Word of God. However, our peace will not be restricted to our understanding because God is never limited in this way:

*"And the peace of God, which surpasses all
understanding, will guard your hearts and minds
in Christ Jesus."* [19]

For those Christians who genuinely fear that the mind can only be an obstacle to faith and revelation I hope that I am demonstrating, from the Bible, that the Christian mind is potentially of great use to God. Because the mind is also the main battlefield for Satan's attacks on the Christian, sometimes the disciple of Christ may suspect the mind of being only an obstacle to holiness. But if Satan can exploit the mind can God not use it even more?

Renewing The Mind

As we have seen, the new birth and regeneration of the mind are essential transformative processes. God commands us in His word to be renewed in our minds. He has not commanded us to change without providing the means to do so. One of these means of renewal is the set of gifts and spiritual attributes given by the Holy Spirit. Another is the washing and *"nourishing"* of our minds by God's Word[20]. A third is our new, living relationship with God, who delivers and heals our minds. From Him we also receive revelation, understanding and grace. As we continue to obey God we grow to discern the voice of the Holy Spirit. We receive new power and discipline over what "comes into" the mind. And the mind that is renewed will worship God, as it focuses on Him.

Now let us look at two key passages that explain this process of renewing the mind. They are 2 Timothy 1:3-7 and Romans 11:33 - 12:2. In the Second Timothy passage, Paul encourages his young protégé, who suffers from timidity (who wouldn't, working with Paul?). This prevailing frailty of fear is very troubling to Timothy; Paul speaks in verse 4 of Timothy's tears. In verses 5-6 Paul encourages the younger man by reminding him that God has called him and that he must rekindle the gift that he had received from the Holy Spirit through the laying on of hands. In verse 7 Paul's language is even more specific: Timothy has not received a spirit of fear (*deilia* "cowardice") from God but rather he has received a new spirit, of *"power"* (*dunameos*), *"love"* (*agapes*) and a *"sound, renewed and right thinking mind"* (*sophronizo*). These three attributes of Timothy's spirit, given by God's Spirit, are manifest in and through all disciples of Christ. We tend to emphasise one or other of these attributes but God wants us all to receive the new spirit that contains all of these qualities and holds them in proper balance; for example, power without love and a sound mind can be dangerous rather than beneficial. Note that this new spirit within the Christian disciple, if we choose to live by and in it, will cancel out the former, negative, attributes that would hold us back from serving God. If we, like Timothy, have received the Holy Spirit then we already have a spirit of power, love and a sound mind. We do not need to ask for something we already possess: we just need to believe that we have it.

In Romans 11:33 – Romans 12:2 we have a very precise reference to the renewed mind. In response to his statements about the inscrutable nature of God in Romans 11:33-34 (*"How unsearchable are His judgements..."* and, *"Who has known the mind of the Lord?"*), Paul states that the only appropriate attitude is one of worship, *"To Him be glory for ever"* (v.35). We cannot understand God with our human minds but as we worship we receive revelation, and by revelation we grow in understanding. In Romans 12:1 Paul begins this next set of thoughts with a *"therefore"*. This means that what he is about to say is as a consequence of the wonderful grace of God explained in the previous chapters and also of the unsearchable nature of God mentioned just before the *"therefore"*. *"Therefore"* each Christian should *"present"* his or her body as a *"living sacrifice"*. *"Present"* according to Josephus is the technical term for offering a sacrifice but this acceptable sacrifice does not require us to die in the physical sense. Our one, true sacrifice, Jesus, has already died for us on the cross. Rather, our own sacrifice is to be a living one, of complete surrender of our wills to God. Part of this surrender involves a conscious and repeated decision not to *"conform"* to the world: not to be shaped by the world's patterns of values, thoughts and beliefs. Rather, we are to be *"transformed"* (*metamorphoo*, to be transfigured from the inside out) by the *"renewal of your mind"*. This latter phrase speaks of a "new" mind, not a repaired, old one. The tense of key verbs implies that this is done *to* us by an active Holy Spirit, as we willingly submit. If God wants to renew our minds He must have a purpose for them!

The process described in such detail in Romans 12:1-2 is of much practical help to the Christian who wants to have a mind freed from the influence of this world (including the "big, dangerous ideas" of Chapter 5), and who wants his or her mind to be filled with godly thoughts and impulses. Let us pray these verses over our minds and expect God to accomplish the renewal that He commands. Each of us should make these promises personal! This is a process – we will still experience battles in our minds (especially when we decide to follow God fully). Remember, losing one battle does not mean we have lost the war! God promises victory to those who overcome through Him. There is every hope for us that, as we surrender fully to God, His Spirit will accomplish this work in us.

This renewal is an essential preparation for the encouragements to come in the remaining verses of Romans Chapter 12 and throughout the next four chapters of Romans. These passages include instructions on ministry, godly attitudes and so on. Without a renewed mind, none of these wonderful benefits and responsibilities would be possible, neither could our lives be pleasing to God.

One of the key purposes God has for renewing our minds is to "write"[21] His laws upon them. This means that the desire of God is to take the regenerate, renewed mind and make it fit for the reception of His truth, communicated to us through revelation by the Holy Spirit.

In this way the renewed mind is enabled to hold that revelation and know it by faith, with the result that it becomes a part of the individual disciple's nature. God wants us to think and to feel righteously, so that our behaviour can be motivated by the values of His Kingdom.

Another aspect of the renewed mind is the change that must be made to the *contents* of the mind. Before coming to Christ the human mind is full of all kinds of "rubbish". This rubbish needs to be cleared out and replaced with edifying mental contents:

> *"In conclusion, my brothers and sisters, fill your minds with those things that are good and that deserve praise: things that are true, noble, right, pure, lovely and honourable."* [22]

What excellent instruction! The mind that is filled with these things will know righteousness, peace and joy in the Holy Spirit.

So, the renewed mind is empowered, in Christ, to say "no" to sin; out of a conviction inspired by God's light (truth, revelation, Scriptures). Conversely, it can say "yes" to every righteous inspiration. The renewed mind steadily considers evil thoughts as temptations – originating from the devil - and it views thoughts of righteousness as daily, even momentary, instances of God's light shining upon and within the mind. This is all the result of God's mercy:

> *"He rescued us from the power of darkness and brought us safe into the kingdom of His dear Son, by whom we are set free, that is, our sins are forgiven."* [23]

As we consider ourselves "dead" to sin we block off every "landing strip" in our minds to the influence of the devil, whose thoughts may circle our minds but need never to be allowed to "land". Again, may I emphasise that what we have been freely given in Christ will need to be outworked as a process of increasing liberty from bondage to undesirable, compulsive thoughts. Truly, it is for freedom that we are now free in our renewed minds! This is what I take the New Testament to mean by "self-control" and obedience. These are the evidences of the outworking of what Christ has given to us, through His work of atonement, when we willingly surrender to the truth of God in our minds, hearts and spirits. This is never achieved merely by human effort but only by the gracious work of the Holy Spirit within the believer.

Revelation and The Mind

Although revelation is central to New Testament teaching it tends either to be a neglected subject or is seen as the sole preserve of the mystic. The word can conjure up mental pictures of an eccentric, "prophet" figure who lives on a strange diet in a wilderness; who will occasionally appear before a gathering of others to issue dire divine warnings and then disappear again into his mysterious solitude. Actually, all Christians are brought to God because of revelation, and revelation will continue to form an essential part of our *"abiding in Christ"*. We cannot walk the path of truth without on-going revelations from the Holy Spirit. Indeed, Jesus tells us, in John 15:15-16 that the hallmark of His "friend" is one who fellowships with Him and hears all that He passes on from the Father. Revelation, like any other aspect of Christianity, can be abused but it is vital to our continuing prayer lives and walk with God.

The English word "revelation" is a translation of the Greek word *apokalupsis*, which means "uncovering". It is like the drawing back of the curtain on a stage, to reveal something that is already there, but which is new and marvellous to the enlightened eye and mind. A powerful symbolic example of this is found in the Gospel of Mark (15:38) when the Temple veil was torn from the top (God's "end") to the bottom (man's "end") as a consequence of Christ's crucifixion. Thus God ushered in the New Testament, superseding yet fulfilling the Old, based entirely upon a heavenly act of gracious atonement:

> *"And we know that the Son of God has come and*
> *has given us understanding so that we may know*
> *Him who is true; and we are in Him who is true,*

in His Son Jesus Christ. He is the true God and eternal life" [24]

Two other analogies can be helpful when explaining revelation. Imagine you are walking along a remote country road on a pitch-dark night. You cannot see anything and the night is still and silent. Suddenly, there is a flash of lightning or car headlights sweep along the road and, in a moment, you see everything that was already there but which was previously obscured by the darkness. The second analogy is of the old fashioned light-exposure photographic plate. The light (revelation) exposes the picture which is then "held" by the plate (so that prints can be taken off it). In the same way, God's revelation is "held" by the renewed mind, which can then faithfully communicate it.

That last point is critical for our consideration of the renewed mind. How often has God revealed a promise or truth to someone only for that person to "lose sight" of it within days? The key is to have that truth, that revelation, held in the renewed mind, like an image held on an old photographic plate. It then becomes an integral part of our understanding of God. I must stress, again, that the work of the Holy Spirit in revelation is to reveal to the individual that which is new for her or him but which has always been true and has already been received by others before us. Beware of those who claim to have "revelation" of things completely unsupported by the Bible, and which no one in church history has ever taught.

Revelation by the Holy Spirit, then, gives us instantaneous understanding of an aspect of God, or of His truth formerly concealed from, or misunderstood by us. Our reception of revelation from the Holy Spirit, from God, because of the atoning work of Christ, is in itself a transformative experience, as we put our faith in His revealed truth. The truth will *"make you free"* as it is revealed to you by the Holy Spirit!

When we pray for or speak to non-believers we must appreciate that they, too, need revelation. The god of this world blinds the eyes of the unbeliever (2 Corinthians 4:4). The unbeliever lives in a state of spiritual blindness. However, the God of all light opens the spiritual eyes of all who come to Him through Christ.

Now let us look at two passages in the Bible, in a little depth, to help our understanding of what biblical revelation is. In 1 Corinthians 2:10-16 the interaction between the believer's spirit and mind is explored. Verse 10 shows us that revelation begins all spiritual processes and that it is the Holy Spirit who searches the *"deep things of God"* on our behalf. He is the only one who can comprehend God (v.11) and it is this same Spirit who has regenerated our spirits and minds, if we are in Christ (v.12). In verse13 we are to (mentally) understand the truths spiritually received, because of illumination by the Holy Spirit. By then we are enlightened, so we can understand and communicate spiritual truths clearly *"by the Spirit"*. In the next verse we see that the natural man cannot understand or receive the gifts of the Spirit; and in verse 15 the man who is enlightened by the Holy Spirit has a renewed faculty for judging all things, which men of natural intellectual talents are incapable of judging. In verse 16 Paul states that the spiritual man is superior to the proud intellectual who attempts even to instruct God! We (those in Christ) now have *"the mind of Christ"*. This is a mind worth having! By continual revelation of God's truth, given by the Holy Spirit, our minds can be transformed as our faculties of judgement, reason, imagination and wisdom are refined. The gift of revelation *reveals* the mind of Christ and as we embrace and hold this revelation we increasingly *have* the mind of Christ.

The second Bible passage is Ephesians 1:15-23. The context of this passage is explained in part in verse 13, which speaks of the revelation of truth, of our faith, of the body of Christ and of grace gifts. Verses 15-23 record a wonderful prayer by Paul for the Christians in Ephesus (it is a good model for our own prayers). Just to focus for a moment on his prayer for revelation, let us look at verses 17-18. In verse 17 Paul prays that they might receive *"a spirit of wisdom and revelation"*, that is, a spirit endowed with *sophias* and *apokalupseos*. This wisdom and revelation should focus on *"the knowledge of Him"* (remember this phrase in Chapter 5 on "big, dangerous ideas"). The *Logos*, the *Alpha* and *Omega* (Christ) is the source and focus of all revelation and wisdom.

Paul goes on to praise God for the Ephesians' common revelation, in verse 18, and to pray for further revelation for them, that *"the eyes of our hearts having been enlightened, you will be enabled to know.."*. Paul prays that they might receive a revelation of hope, riches and power. Note the *"our"* and the past tense for the common work of Christ in them all; this is followed by the *"you"* and the use of the future tense for a revelation of knowledge already gained by Paul but not, as yet, by them.

There is a simple but profound verse near the end of Luke's gospel that should give hope to all who want deeper insights into God's Word:

> *"Then opened He their understanding, that they*
> *might understand the scriptures"* [25]

If you need greater revelation of God and of His truth, then ask for it, spend time with Him and expect to receive it. In general and specific terms, you can and should ask God to reveal Himself and His truth to you more and more. Furthermore, you can ask Him to enable you to "hold" what He has shown you, in your renewed mind.

Or, perhaps you have never "known" God personally? I vividly remember my first prayer to Him, as an agnostic. It ran something like: "God, if you are there, please reveal yourself to me". Hardly the most inspired or faith-filled prayer ever! But God, in His great grace and mercy, revealed Himself to me. In the weeks before I became a Christian, I became increasingly aware of a darkness around me and within me that prevented me from seeing God. Then, on the night when I became a Christian, revelation played a key part in my conversion. I "saw" and experienced the truth and presence of God for the first time. This revelation transformed my life. Furthermore, by God's grace only, His truth moved me from revelation to increasing understanding and then to conviction. This side of heaven we can only ever know "in part" but our knowledge of Him can increase, and that knowledge is changing our lives for the better.

Finally, it is important to remember that revelation and faith are not the same as "positive thinking". There are those who argue that in order to prosper all you need to do is to think positive thoughts, based on your own imagination or desires. There are also Christians for whom faith has become an end in itself or a formula by which we wring out of God whatever we want. Christian faith and revelation have, as their focus, God Himself and His revealed will. The key is: what are we putting our faith in? Is it our positive thinking and faith, or God's character and truth? Revelation uncovers a truth previously hidden from us and faith is thus inspired. So, as we *"set our minds"* on the things that are above, where God is, we find revelation, faith and peace. We also grow in the knowledge of God.

The Battlefield of The Mind

As we have seen, Ephesians 1:18-19 contains a prayer by Paul for the mature group of Christians in Ephesus. It expresses and implies some striking promises by God for the believer. Firstly, the prayer indicates that some of us Christians lack the revelation for which Paul prays, or he would have no need to pray for it. Secondly, there is clearly a common problem of "holding" revelation that is received, (as discussed before) so that it becomes a part of our understanding, faith and character.

This problem of "holding" revelation is also expressed in another prayer in Ephesians, beginning in Chapter 3:18. In this prayer, Paul prays that the Ephesian Christians may have *"full strength"* to lay hold of God's love effectively *"with the mind"* – a love that would otherwise be incomprehensible to the human soul. Why pray like this? Partly because we need God's strength and grace to receive revelation, when it comes. Mainly, though, this prayer is necessary because the mind is the major spiritual battleground in our lives. In this context look at Revelation 2:4.

We shall see, in the next chapter, how Satan seeks to sow seeds of doubt in the believer's mind (as he did with Adam and Eve) and that he tries very hard to entice us with "big, dangerous ideas", as well as with more personal temptations. Ephesians 6 dramatically illustrates the nature of the Christian life, portraying it as one of constant wrestling (by the way, ancient wrestling was far from fake entertainment – it was bloody and sometimes lethal) with various spirits, demons and fallen angels that attack our bodies, emotions and minds. Just as we see in Genesis, the devil's ultimate goal in this "wrestling match" is to persuade us to deny our faith in God.

Let us now look at an Old Testament example of the spiritual battle described above. This narrates the dramatic and instructive story of Elijah and Jezebel. The drama begins with Elijah's victory on Mount Carmel, a victory won through the ferocious and unflinching faith of the prophet. Could anything sway a man of God of this calibre? No one is immune from severe spiritual attack or counter-attack! This is especially true of those who are actively seeking or serving God, or who have just won a spiritual victory. In 1 Kings 19:2-18 we witness the power and effectiveness of the devil's counter-attack. Remember, the devil will try to attack us all in similar ways, so we can all learn from Elijah's experiences. In verse 2 we can read Jezebel's curse, which "releases" a savage demonic assault on Elijah (notice that, although there are physical threats, the main assault comes against Elijah's mind and feelings). In verse 3 one of the mightiest men of God in the Old Testament is gripped with such powerful terror that he begins to act out of fear rather than faith. By verse 4 he exhibits the classic signs of depression: anxiety, isolation, listlessness, brooding, despair and thoughts of suicide. By now the spiritual enemy of Elijah, defeated on Mount Carmel and seeking revenge, has wormed his way fully into the prophet's mind. By now the devil has fully convinced Elijah of his lies.

What was the internal weakness in the prophet that gave the devil this "toe-hold"? In verse 10 we see that self-pity or pride was the avenue that Satan used to gain an almost fatal entrance into Elijah's mind. Elijah had convinced himself that he was the only one really serving God ("...*I, even I only, am left; and they seek my life, to take it away*" cf v.14). We are reminded that, even before his great Mount Carmel triumph, Elijah had stated the same (false) perception – in 1 Kings 18:22 he declared to the assembled people that he was the only one remaining who was faithful to God. Both in triumph and depression Elijah was convinced of this lie. When God revealed to him that there were actually 7,000 others who had remained faithful to Jehovah, the prophet began to bring a godly perspective to the raging battle in his mind, and from verses 5(b) to 18 his relationship with God was gradually restored through God's gracious physical, spiritual, emotional and mental healing. By the end of the passage Elijah was restored and was once more ready for the fight!

Part of a New Testament parable, in Luke 8:5, is also very relevant and instructive in this respect. In an extended picture of spiritual truth, taken from a farming scene, Jesus speaks of good seed being sown on three types of soil. Notice in the Matthew 13:19 version of the parable, the resistant paths represent those who do not *"understand"* the message of the Kingdom of God, those, in other words, who do not receive or accept the Holy Spirit's revelation of the truth. As soon as the *"seed"* (God's Word or revelation) is sown into a life that is hard or resistant the next visitor to the field (a picture of the individual human heart and mind) is a black bird, which attempts to steal it. Even if we are willing to receive, then hold the seed of revelation, we often have to wrestle to keep it, as we see with the example of Elijah.

How do we win this battle? Fundamental to victory is a series of truths revealed in James 1:5-8. God tells us, through James, that we are to see doubt as the enemy of faith. We are to listen humbly to God, to hear from Him, and having heard from Him to be fully persuaded that He is able to do what He has promised. In Romans 4:18-22 we receive more exhortation. True faith is to trust in the revealed will of God, whether or not we fully understand it at the beginning. Faith sees God as mightier than all obstacles to the fulfilment of His promises. Faith takes us beyond our prior experience, our resources and ability. Faith does not entertain doubt, it is the unwavering conviction that God will deliver on His promises because He is utterly trustworthy. Victory is guaranteed, provided that our faith is based on God's will, truth and resources - not on our own ideas or abilities:

> *"Wherefore take unto you the whole armour of God, that ye may be able to withstand in the evil day, and having done all, to stand."* [26]

Part of the *"having done all, to stand"* is to do what Colossians 3:2 commands:

> *"Keep your minds fixed on the things there [heaven], not on the things here on earth."* [27]

Remember how Satan works. He attempts to plant a doubt, a temptation or a deceit in your mind – hoping that you will believe it and act upon it. Whether you act upon it or not, he will attempt to condemn you for having had the thought in the first place. The devil is the Accuser of the Brethren. Not all evil thoughts begin with him but many do. How should we respond when we recognise a thought that does not belong in the Christian mind? We must *"take every thought captive"* to Christ and refuse to be condemned, if there is nothing to repent of. We should repent and receive God's forgiveness if we need to. Throughout our Christian lives, in every way and at all times, we must remember that our enemy is not "flesh and blood". Avoid conflict with fellow Christians and, if at all possible, live in peace with all men. Our enemy is spiritual and he can only be overcome with the mighty spiritual weapons given to us by God:

> *"And they have conquered him by the blood of the Lamb and by the word of their testimony, for they loved not their lives even unto death."* [28]

The *"him"* who is overcome in this verse is Satan, the Accuser of the Brethren. How is he overcome? By confessing what the blood of Christ has achieved for us; and by valuing the desire to please God more highly than life itself.

CHAPTER 5

PATHWAYS OF DECEPTION
(BIG, DANGEROUS IDEAS)

*"Go in through the narrow gate, because the gate
to hell is wide and the road that leads to it is easy,
and there are many who travel it."* [1]

Introduction

When I first became a Christian, God impressed upon me the importance of believing the Bible to be the only divinely inspired, infallible book. I was to believe it and take its promises literally – when the Holy Spirit demonstrated that these promises applied to me. The Bible changes us: we do not change it. In our contemporary societies in the West, the Bible's authority has come under increasing scrutiny and criticism. If it is indeed the truth that makes us free, then we must understand what the Bible itself says about the nature of truth and its warnings about the attempts of a very clever devil to undermine it, using deception as his most powerful weapon.

Having discussed the battlefield of the mind, in our previous chapter,

I now want us to consider some very influential deceptions, which I call "big, dangerous ideas". They are "big" because they are widely believed to be the truth, and they are "dangerous" because they conflict with the truth of the Bible. In our contemporary period - both at an individual and at a social level – orthodox Christianity is being challenged by many powerful intellectual, ethical, moral and spiritual ideas.

There is nothing new about forceful spiritual, moral and intellectual opposition to Christianity. Two core Christian beliefs that faced particularly hostile challenges, during the period of the post-Apostolic church, were the nature and status of Christ and the canon and authority of the Bible. These two issues of faith are and will continue to be key subjects for attacks against Christianity during our own age. I believe that, as the Church approaches the end of this age, opposition to its beliefs will intensify. Already, in "Christian" nations across Europe, it has become politically incorrect to mention Christ by name. Moreover, the moral authority of the Bible has come to be questioned in an almost unprecedented manner. Those who believe in the inspired authority of the Bible are now sneeringly labelled by many as "fundamentalists".

These twin attacks are, according to the Bible, set to intensify in the future. The New Testament predicts that antagonism to the truth of God will be a key sign of the "Last Days":

> "Remember that there will be difficult times in the last days. People…will hold to the outward form of our religion, but reject its real power… As Jannes and Jambres [Egyptian sorcerers] were opposed to Moses, so also these people are opposed to the truth…" [2]

The Greek word *chalepos*, translated in the Good News Bible as "*difficult*", means "furious" or "fierce". This word is rarely used in the New Testament. On another occasion it refers to the "fierce" behaviour of the Gadarene demoniacs[3]. Make no mistake about it, there will be a period of time before the return of Christ when there will be open, demonically inspired hostility towards orthodox, biblical Christianity.

Some argue that this period of open aggression towards Christianity has already begun. Furthermore, the reference to Jannes and Jambres in this passage warns us of a false religion that will rise up in violent opposition to the truth of the Gospel, before the return of Christ.

Having considered the past and the future, let us look briefly at the present. The Bible is commonly ignored, doubted or criticised in today's Western societies. Often this is because alternative philosophies or ideas seem to be more modern, relevant, convenient or plausible. This is especially true when these philosophies seem to provide modern explanations for issues that had previously been settled in Christian teaching throughout its 2,000 year history. Such fashionable beliefs have become the "truth" for many because they are promoted by the media and have consequently helped to shape the popular values and the dominant belief systems of the main institutions of Western states. This means that they appear to modern, Western societies, at first glance, to be more "relevant" than biblical teaching. How does the Bible explain the origins of these persuasive philosophies and ideas? How relevant is its teaching today, in the face of this tremendous onslaught by these "big, dangerous ideas"? If we are to discount these popular, plausible philosophies then what are we to believe, in their place?

Despite the growth of secularism and materialism in the West, individuals and nations still seek some spiritual star by which to steer. However, all too often the Bible is rejected as an outdated, "unloving" and superstitious work of fiction, or it is re-interpreted to suit modern tastes, theories and ethics. Many non-Christians have been persuaded by the common fallacy that the Bible is no more than a controversial, historical document. People in the West are also influenced by a widely held belief that all spiritual teaching is ultimately an issue of personal choice or interpretation. Such a belief rejects the exclusive claim by the Bible that it communicates absolute truth, divinely inspired, which must be accepted or rejected in its entirety. Indeed, many in the West now look upon personal belief systems with the consumerist view that such a system is something each individual designs to suit their own taste – a kind of moral and religious "pick-'n-mix" exercise. Many also believe, as I once did, that Christian beliefs merely form a "crutch" for the weak and ignorant.

Before I became a Christian I also rejected the teaching of the Bible as so much old-fashioned superstition: "How could any intelligent person believe in its claims?" is what I would have said then. What a joy it was to discover, over thirty years ago, the riches of truth revealed to me through its pages, lit by the revelation of the Holy Spirit. Through all the ups and downs of life during the intervening years I have never doubted the unique claims and power of the Word of God. I have never been disappointed in this trust.

The Origin and Purpose of Non-Christian Beliefs

As we have already discussed, convincing ideas come together to form pathways for life's journey. The routes we take and the decisions we make throughout our lives tend to be based on our core values and beliefs. It is my intention in this chapter to identify some of the pathways that are very popular and crowded but which – for the Christian – are pathways of total or partial deception. These pathways – philosophies, popular beliefs or value systems – are very coherent and enticing but they lead the individual who follows them away from the God of the Christian Bible. Some of them very obviously offer alternative views to those of the Bible. Other pathways are like forks on the pathway of truth – they appear at first to diverge only marginally from orthodox Christian truth but the further the path is taken the wider is the gulf that grows between it and the Narrow Way that leads to salvation. Is there a common source for these very diverse pathways of deception? What does the Bible have to say about them?

Behind most determined, conscious actions lie ideas. Ideas motivate actions and most individual, political and social behaviours. They are more powerful than any weapon devised by man, as men will die *for* them as well as *because of* them. When ideas come together to form religions, philosophies, or moral attitudes these become pathways for the mind or soul: pathways that will lead to truth or error. The enticing pathways of deception will always end in tears, as Proverbs 14:12 warns us:

"What you think is the right road may lead to death."[4]

According to the Bible there are only three possible sources for any idea: God, the devil or the human mind. By contrast, according to the common Western worldview there is no such thing as the spiritual or the supernatural – or if there is it is ultimately unknowable. Despite this scepticism every human being has a sense of the spiritual or the transcendent, no-matter how dulled this sense may be.

Paul states, in 2 Corinthians 10:3-4, that though Christians live in the physical world we carry out a powerful, spiritual warfare against spiritual "strongholds". Paul clearly believed, in harmony with Christ's teaching, that the spiritual and material worlds affect each another profoundly, indeed Paul attributes much of what happens on planet earth to spiritual sources and human responses to them. In ancient warfare strongholds were mountainous fortifications that were notoriously difficult to overcome. They were built by an occupying military force, after this force had gained geographical, military or political advantage in a nation or region. The strongholds described by Paul in 2 Corinthians 10:3-4 are spiritual in nature and origin. They manifest themselves as increasingly popular ideas that take people away from the true knowledge of God. He dramatically describes this spiritual battle, in verses 4-5:

> *"We destroy false arguments; we pull down every*
> *proud obstacle that is raised against the knowledge*
> *of God; we take every thought captive and make*
> *it obey Christ."*[5]

Here Paul envisages a necessary spiritual war by Christians against big, powerful, popular and dangerous arguments, set up by Satan to oppose the true knowledge of God. These arguments take such a hold in a society or nation that they are described as "strongholds".

I see these ideas as "big and dangerous" because they offer popular but non-biblical explanations for the human condition. They have enormous popularity because they appeal in many ways to basic human needs or desires. They thereby invade the world of ideas, set up "strongholds" and take and hold emotional, intellectual and spiritual territory. They begin, like a small invasion force, as radical, minority views but they eventually come to be accepted as received truth, having conquered the thinking of a nation or society. They constitute one of the devil's key strategies to lead men away from the knowledge of God. These ideas or belief systems are coherent and apparently logical. In other words they seem to make a lot of sense, or they would not be so convincing. Their main appeal, however, lies in their attractiveness to basic human passions and desires.

In Ephesians 6:10-11, Paul asserts that our enemy is an organised force of intelligent, demonic personalities led by Satan. Many of their attacks come in the form of clever ideas and schemes ("*wiles*"). Paul goes on to argue that this army can only be overcome by the Christian's use of spiritual weapons. No amount of cleverness on our part will overcome their demonic intelligence. A leading group of powerful spirits in Satan's army, identified in verse 12, are the "*world rulers of this present darkness*", ("*darkness*" often symbolises, in the Bible, a wilful ignorance or denial of God). I take these "*world rulers*" to be powerful, fallen angels with a special remit to deepen and extend the world's spiritual darkness, by generating popular ideas that lead mankind away from a knowledge of God.

In 2 Corinthians 11:14 Paul states that:

> "…*Satan himself masquerades as an angel of light*" [6]

Here "*light*" is used ironically of Satan's deceptive lies, which appear truthful but which are, in fact, a disguise to tempt the unwary into following an illusion of the truth. Satan's "*light*" is presented as a tempting array of philosophies, of big, dangerous ideas that entice the individual on to a path away from his or her loving Father. These ideas are "big" in that they eventually influence or dominate a society's consciousness to a point when they are accepted as "normal", or are widely believed to be the "truth". They find their way into all branches of the media and into every social activity. They are "dangerous" because they are appealing lies, masquerading as light, misleading multitudes.

These ideas seek to make God and the knowledge of Him appear outdated, irrelevant and illogical. They can ultimately shape individual human consciousness. In other words, they can determine how we see ourselves and how we view God. As a result of their source and because of their content, these ideas argue against *"the knowledge of God"*. According to Paul our task, as Christians, is to discern these ideas and overcome them by taking them *"captive"* to Christ. Equally, we should be aware that they attempt to take Christians captive – away from a true knowledge of God and along pathways, falsely lit, that will lead, ultimately, to spiritual darkness.

One example is particularly revealing. It is the devil's attempt to conceal his very existence. Many today will view any literal belief in demons, Satan and demonically inspired ideas as just so much superstition. These subjects are not often taught in many churches. And where they are taught, they are often taught in terms of modern thinking informed by psychology, sociology and so on – broadly speaking, that evil is abstract (it is a "thing" not a personality) and that there are no such creatures as a literal devil or literal demons. So, according to many, there is no intelligent source of evil. The problem for those who profess to be Christians and who wish to argue this, is that Jesus clearly believed in the existence of the devil and of demons. He cast demons out of people and encouraged His followers to cast them out also. He also resisted the devil in the wilderness. This is not to say that there is no room for a combination of spiritual, medical and counselling therapies to be prayerfully applied, according to the needs of each person. However, we see in the passages quoted above (from 2 Corinthians and Ephesians) that Paul also describes fallen angels as real, personal, intelligent enemies of the Christian.

In this chapter I will discuss some of the most common ideas that have come to dominate popular Western thinking during the past century. The list is necessarily incomplete. I intend to consider these ideas in the popular forms that give them common expression and meaning in most people's minds and conversations, rather than examine them as academic theories. Set against these pathways of popular beliefs and philosophies are the radical and exclusive claims of Christ, which are forever unique and exclusive:

> *"I am the way, the truth, and the life; no one goes*
> *to the Father except by me."* [7]

We must all begin our journey of truth by believing that God exists; and that the only pathway to God is through Christ. Anything that teaches otherwise is, by definition, error.

Atheism

We begin our consideration of "big, dangerous ideas" by briefly examining the belief that is most obviously at odds with *the knowledge of God*. The contemporary definition of "atheism" describes it as a firmly held conviction that there is no God and that people who believe in a god (or gods) are deluded. Actually, there are more agnostics (people who are unsure whether God exists, or not) in the West than there are convinced atheists, who have been estimated to number around 4% of the world's population. A Western atheist's view of the world is often based on a kind of scientific rationalism, which holds that everything that cannot be proven, intellectually, is at best a theory and at worst a deception.

This modern meaning of atheism is not to be confused with the Romans' understanding of the word *atheist*, which they used to justify the persecution of Christians. They considered atheists to be worshippers of the "wrong" god, or those who failed to worship the "true" gods.

Modern atheism is essentially a belief system that, despite its inability to disprove God's existence, would argue that the responsibility lies with Christians to "prove" the existence of God. As a belief system, atheism has its own texts, apologists, saints and preachers but it appears to be declining in numbers. The more enduring impact of atheism has been its spawning of a general corrosive scepticism, that has increasingly eaten into Western societies' traditional belief in the Christian God. In our own period, in the West, despite its most recent decline, atheist beliefs have had an enormous influence on politics, all arms of government, education and the media. This makes it difficult, in these and other fields of human activity, to express our Christian faith without being derided.

The greatest appeal of atheism is that, in the absence of an all-powerful God, human beings – either as individuals or groups – can invent their own individual or group moral codes. These morals, they believe, are conveniently not subject to judgement by a holy God. This is an extremely attractive proposition for people of any age but perhaps it holds a special appeal for our own materialistic, egocentric and permissive era.

Another tactic of those who promote atheism is to argue that religious belief is more than a mere harmless fantasy: it is actually dangerous. In the view of some atheists, many wars have been started by religious individuals, groups or nations who have sought to expand or impose their beliefs by force of arms. The Crusades, for example, are often cited by those who criticise "fanatical" Christianity as a damning example of the aggressiveness of deluded religious adherents. However, any objective study of the Crusades must conclude that the version of Christianity held by the Crusader leaders was quite foreign to the teaching of the New Testament. Furthermore, it has also been persuasively argued that religion was – to some extent at least - simply a useful *casus belli*, a convincing propaganda tool to excuse colonising ambitions and to motivate individuals to give their lives for an ultimately futile political and economic cause. Pope Urban's reasons and motives for calling the First Crusade are a matter for debate and speculation but to portray them as purely "religious" is to over-simplify a fascinating yet complicated period of European and Middle-Eastern history. That the Crusades were inspired by a wicked distortion of Christian teaching; that they were disastrous for relations between Islam and Christianity, and that they were bloodthirsty and cruel is all beyond dispute. Actually, far from being the aggressors, it has been estimated by some that up to seventy million Christians have been martyred for their faith since the crucifixion of Christ (about 65% of them since 1900). Christians, many of whom are citizens of atheistic states, are currently detained in prisons or they are being executed or tortured for their faith.

Atheism has its roots in ancient philosophy but it only emerged as a popular modern belief system in the West during the Enlightenment of the seventeenth and eighteenth centuries. This was when a number of very influential thinkers argued persuasively against traditional Christian beliefs. It expressed itself most violently (before the twentieth century) during the French Revolution, when disillusionment with the perceived injustices of the Catholic Church inspired a popular form of atheism, which violently persecuted Christianity. However, this opposition to formal Christianity was soon abandoned in France by Napoleon Bonaparte when he considered it useful to seek the involvement of the Pope during his coronation as Emperor.

During the mid-to-late nineteenth century four highly influential thinkers emerged in Europe, three of whom believed that the real battleground on which religious beliefs would be legitimately fought and vanquished, was the battleground of ideas and communication. Their beliefs would contribute, directly or indirectly, to the anti-religious revolutions and movements of the next century. These men's publications were so influential that religious beliefs came increasingly to be identified with irrational delusions and wish-fulfilments, or even with the suppression of the poor and ignorant. They popularised the belief that man had invented God because man needed Him to exist!

These four thinkers' publications, intentionally or otherwise, added fuel to the impetus towards atheism becoming an acceptable belief system. They were: in science, Darwin's *Origin of The Species* (1859); in religious philosophy, Feuerbach's *The Essence of Christianity* (1841); in social history and political theory, Marx's *Communist Manifesto* (1848); and in psychology Freud's theories about psychogenesis (the psychological reasons for beginnings, for example, the source of religious faith). All four thinkers had an enormous individual and collective negative impact upon the common acceptance of Christian beliefs.

Darwin himself saw no necessary contradiction between his theory of evolution and faith in a Divine Being, however, it is the use to which

Darwin's ideas have been put by supporters of atheism that concerns us more here. The Theory of Evolution affords an opportunity for those who wish to argue against Creationism – it offers a godless explanation of the material universe. Atheism, when combined with the Theory of Evolution, consigns man to an accidental, meaningless existence. Spiritual significance is thereby rejected and man is reduced to the level of an intelligent animal.

It is fair to summarise the impact of these four thinkers as (intentionally or otherwise) enormously popularising atheism and various other forms of humanism. What was faith in a Divine Being to be replaced with? Why, knowledge of course! Does this sound familiar? The process of the erosion of Christian faith in the West was aided, in the late nineteenth century, by the increasingly liberal approach to Christian theology that was taken in many universities and seminaries. This approach came to be known as Higher Criticism.

Feuerbach's view of Christianity provides an example of the influence of these four men on popular religious beliefs. Feuerbach argued that God was a delusion, invented by mankind as a kind of wish-fulfilment, and that organised religion exploited this delusion and perpetuated it for the benefit of the clergy, at the expense of the ordinary people. Moreover, Feuerbach argued that this delusion created universal human guilt. Religion also served, he argued, to excuse the painful life of servitude and the grinding poverty experienced by the mass of the peoples of Europe. It excused this present suffering by promising a future, eternal life of bliss in the hereafter. The proper replacement for religious myth, Feuerbach and others argued, was the scientific or revolutionary pursuit of truth and social justice. In turn, Marx developed political and Freud psychological theories based on the premise that God is an invention of the human mind.

When we consider the first half of the twentieth century the impact of these thinkers can be seen. One example was in the growing popularity and near-veneration of science, which seemed to offer rational explanations for the Big Questions. By the 1950s, in the West, there was a widespread belief that science could solve all of man's problems, and compensate for moral decadence by inventing "cures" for various ills. In

Marx's case, his theories had an enormous impact upon many nations around the world as communist states, between 1917 and 1989, sought to impose atheism by using varying degrees and forms of repression and persecution. However, it is fair to say that the overall atheistic impact of the influential thinkers mentioned above has not been to replace religious faith. Fewer and fewer people see any fundamental conflict between a belief in God and a circumspect regard for scientific research and theory. Moreover, by the mid-1980s Marx's political and social theories had largely been abandoned as politically, socially and economically unworkable.

It is worth adding, at this point, that atheism should not be confused with hostility or indifference towards organised religion. In a 2007 survey, broadcast by the BBC, a large majority of those questioned in England and Wales stated that they rarely (if ever) attend a church service but a significant majority also claimed that they believe that prayer is answered by God. In another poll around half of those asked claimed to believe in God whilst only ten percent claimed to attend church. I believe that this illustrates the fact that more people have a problem with organised religion than they do with holding a belief in God. Despite these figures, faith in God continues to be patronisingly disparaged by a small number of intellectual apologists of atheism, who sarcastically describe religious belief as a form of ignorant delusion.

All predictions by atheists in the first part of the twentieth century, that religion would die away in the latter half of the century, have been proven to be false. I will use just one example to support this conclusion. In post-Maoist China state-sanctioned Bible printers in Nanjing were forced to move to larger premises in 2008, because demand outstripped supply. Bearing in mind that there are many other locations around the world in which Bibles are printed, the figure of fifty million Bibles printed and sold from this factory alone by December 2007 is remarkable. China – which once promoted state atheism - is now exporting Bibles to Russia and Africa!

Nevertheless, in the West, atheism continues to have enormous popular influence, especially when combined with some of the other ideas and philosophies explored in this chapter. Atheism offers a path away from a belief in any god, whether Christian or otherwise. This path inevitably leads to an abyss of ignorance and hopelessness, as it is a path that takes anyone who travels on it away from moral accountability and eternal hope. Thankfully, it is a path taken by a decreasing number of people.

Consumerism and Materialism

This modern, twin set of values has very ancient parents. They are the offspring of ancient hedonistic philosophies directly described in the Bible:

"Take life easy, eat, drink and enjoy yourself!" [8]

As well as the ancient attractions of hedonism (the selfish pursuit of pleasure), more modern aspects of humanism and existentialism can also be detected as the core values of consumerism and materialism. These sets of values appeal to some very basic human instincts: the desire to be happy and popular; to have more than we need (and certainly more than our neighbour has); and to be masters of our own material destinies. The rich man described in Luke 12, who speaks the words quoted above about enjoying himself, has more than he needs so he builds ever larger barns to store his goods. Meanwhile, he is careless not only of the needs of those around him but also of the state of his own soul. Besides, someone else will ultimately inherit and enjoy his wealth! This irony reminds us of a wise observation in Ecclesiastes:

"A man to whom God hath given riches, wealth and honour, so that he wanteth nothing for his soul of all he desireth, yet God giveth him not power to eat thereof, but a stranger eateth it: this is vanity, and it is an evil disease" [9]

This is a sad picture of someone who spends his whole life acquiring more and more money and goods, only to have someone else inherit it all after he is dead or otherwise incapable of enjoying it.

Consumerism and materialism are twin socio-economic philosophies, served by the high priesthood of the advertising industry. They are based on a world of commerce and the purchase of goods or services – many of which, in the Western world, are not essential to life. The key mantra of this belief system is "choice", peddling the illusion that we can have whatever, or as much as we wish (at a price!) and that this never-ending acquisition of money, goods and services will ultimately lead to greater happiness. This can be very appealing on two levels: we all like to think we are in complete control of our lives; and, of course, we like to be better off than others! In the West this philosophy has influenced some erroneous preaching and re-interpretation of Christian doctrine, which seeks to combine service for God with the pursuit of wealth. It is certainly true that poverty is not a blessing for any person or nation but neither is selfish greed masquerading as faith.

As environmental concerns grow and as the world's resources shrink, wasteful forms of conspicuous consumption will go the way of fur coats, as popular opinion in the West swings away from extravagant consumerism. However, greed is a constant of human nature in any historical period, so this root philosophy will continue to hold an appeal. Materialists should be aware of God's opinion of the philosophy portrayed in Luke 12:19-20, where the rich man's folly is exposed by God:

> *"Then I will say to myself, Lucky man! You have all the good things you need for many years. Take life easy, eat, drink, and enjoy yourself! But God said to him, You fool! This very night you will have to give up your life; then who will get all these things you have kept for yourself?"* [10]

In verse 15 of the same chapter, Christ states:

> *"a person's true life is not made up of the things he owns, no matter how rich he may be."* [11]

How wise! Actually, as usual, the New Testament exposes a negative, selfish human attitude and then goes on to direct Christians to positive behaviour – made possible by the transformation of the individual, in Christ. The greed of the rich man illustrated above is in stark contrast with the question posed in 1 John 3:17:

> *"Whoever has this world's goods, and sees his brother in need, and shuts up his heart from him, how does the love of God abide in him?"* [12]

In Romans 12:1 we are instructed to *"offer"* ourselves to God, *"as a living sacrifice"*. A key aspect of this lifelong act of worship is outlined in the next verse:

> *"Do not conform yourselves to the standards of this world, but let God transform you inwardly by a complete change of your mind. Then you will be able to know the will of God – what is good and pleasing to Him and is perfect."* [13]

We are not to have our understanding shaped by the world's values. This includes, for the Christian, a conscious rejection of selfish greed and self-centredness in all of its forms. For the Christian, clothed in Christ, beauty cannot be bought but is given freely by God. The Bible says, three times, *"worship the Lord in the beauty of holiness"*[14.] We cannot purchase holiness in a shop or on the internet!

Another influence of consumerism in Western society can be seen in the attitude of many towards the concept of church. The Christian Church is described in the Bible as the Body of Christ, into which the believer is baptised and to which the believer is committed[15]. The church is the Bride[16] for whom the Bridegroom, Christ, is returning. Sadly, consumerist thinking in the West has, in some cases, turned the local church in many people's minds into a "brand", a "product" or a "service industry". Some business models of church encourage the Church-goer to think of himself as a client, free to criticise the "product" or "service" on offer. This creates a peculiar set of relationships and expectations between the Body of Christ and the individual. The church becomes "them" not "us" and is easily left when a better offer comes along. There are some legitimate reasons for moving church but the "church-hopper" will generally expect others to change, never himself. Churches which consciously seek to offer a pleasing "product" in the interest of "growth" will always create these shallow and transient relations; they may grow numerically for a brief period but they will see little qualitative growth in terms of holiness and self-sacrifice. A "low cost" discipleship will never transform anyone! None of this is to say that the church should be amateurish or disorganised but neither should it surrender core spiritual values on the altars of popular appeal, consumerist or business models of organisation; or of superficial notions of relevance.

Cultural and Social Postmodernism

By Cultural and Social Postmodernism I mean the popular belief that human nature is not shaped or understood by any "story" such as Christianity, which offers an ordered explanation, for example, of the origin and nature of the human condition. Rather, this belief argues that the society, location and historical period into which an individual is born and within which he or she grows will shape his or her behaviour. According to this philosophy there is no plan as such – individuals are influenced by a random set of circumstances. Of course, there is an element of truth in this belief – we are bound to be influenced by the world around us to some extent. Our early, formative years strongly influence the person we become in later life.

But the particular sense in which I wish to consider social postmodernism is in how it differs from the Bible in its understanding of individual human responsibility. Of course, most people do not use terms like "social postmodernism" but you will often hear popular expressions of this and similar philosophies. For example you may hear that "so-and-so was driven to crime because of his deprived upbringing". According to the logic of this theory, the state or "society" becomes responsible for individual human actions. Yet in Britain today, the fourth wealthiest nation in the world, the prisons are very full! It is the duty and privilege of every Christian to help alleviate suffering wherever he or she finds it. Nevertheless, we must not confuse necessary, outward, material help with inner transformation. Neither should we excuse criminal actions in our attempts to understand what has caused them.

The truth is, of course, that no two individuals will react in exactly the same way to the same cultural, social and historical influences. It is not inevitable that deprivation will lead to crime in all cases, nor do all inhabitants of refugee camps become suicide bombers. Even by the logic of observable facts, this philosophy is highly over-rated. There must be other, more potent, influences upon human behaviour? Saints, scholars and scoundrels have emerged from the same sprawling slums – to lead very different lives. What, then, is the appeal of this philosophy?

One of the clearest attractions of postmodernism is that it shifts responsibility for an individual's actions away from the individual, on to their family, society, culture or historical period. Or better still, we can blame the government! Our behaviour becomes the consequence of someone else's failure. So we are always victims: never sinners. Of course, there is some truth in the fact that what others have done – or failed to do - has affected all of us but until each individual takes personal responsibility for his or her own motives, behaviour and actions – and repents of them – there is no hope for real and lasting change. To those Christians who are influenced by this philosophy and thus see the love of God as a form of eternal indulgence towards the Christian or non-Christian I would say, you may be unwittingly robbing the individual of their hope for forgiveness and lasting, inner transformation. As Paul asks:

> *"What, then? Shall we sin, because we are not under the law, but under God's grace? By no means!"* [17]

None of us changes until we see the personal need for change, combined with a hope that our current state can change, moving us to a faith inspired by the promises of God.

This philosophy often portrays orthodox Christianity as "unloving". This is generally *not* because there is a widespread belief that Christianity does not involve itself in practical love for mankind, including good works to aid the "widow and the orphan". The generosity and practical love demonstrated by most Christian churches is widely understood. The "unloving" criticism tends to be levelled at orthodox Christians when certain moral behaviours are identified by them as sinful, according to the Bible. This is an important distinction. Of course, if a church is not practical as well as spiritual in its expression of the Good News it may well need to re-visit the Bible to consider the heart of God towards the weak and oppressed. Furthermore, the Christian church will, or ought to, acknowledge the very real impact of social, familial, inherited and other factors upon the behaviour and circumstances of individuals, in its counselling and discipleship ministries. However, without the conviction that something is wrong, and harmful to others, why should anyone change? Conviction of personal sin is where all meaningful and lasting transformation must begin.

Genetic Determinism

Genetic Determinism is the name increasingly given to the belief that individual identity and behaviour are dictated by our inherited, genetic make-up. According to this philosophy, our destinies are significantly pre-determined by our genes. Technological language is sometimes used to communicate this belief: according to some we are "hard-wired", or "programmed" in certain ways that dictate our behaviour and the directions our lives take.

Recent scientific research into DNA and genetics have put flesh on the bones of the old Nature versus Nurture debate. Are we overwhelmingly the product of our parents' genes? Or are we the product of our environment and training? Put another way, are our lives an outworking of the inevitable consequences of our genes, or are our lives shaped more by what happens to us? And have we any choice in any of this? Most scientists will argue that we are shaped by both genes and environmental factors. According to radical genetic determinism it is our genes, not our wills, (and certainly not God's will or ability) that will "shape" our destinies.

Of course, real and exciting advances in the fields of medicine and bio-chemistry are being made possible due to our increasing knowledge of human genetics. Cures may well be found – as a result of these advances – for diseases that are currently hereditary and debilitating or even terminal. But these advances in knowledge also pose ethical, moral and theological questions, which for the sake of simplicity I will consider as falling into two main categories.

The first category of concerns falls under the heading of *eugenics*: the manipulation of genes, human reproduction - or the choice of who lives or dies – for medical, racial, political, judicial, economic, cosmetic or other reasons. A number of ancient civilisations practised primitive forms of eugenics by exposing unwanted babies on hillsides. In the case of the Spartans, mothers disposed of weak, malformed or even just plain babies by dropping them into a nearby gorge so that the purity and vigour of the native race could be maintained. The location of this socially sanctioned and accepted infanticide (called the *Apothetae*, or "Dumping Ground") is a cleft in the rocks on the mountain road to Messenia. Before we rush to condemnation of the Spartans' barbaric behaviour let us remember that unwanted babies are disposed of, in much greater numbers, in most Western cultures: admittedly this is done more technologically and discreetly nowadays but people still find ample justification for so doing.

One of the most famous examples of the systematic use of eugenics in recent European history was the programme instigated in Germany under Hitler, whereby scientists sought to produce (or "maintain") a pure, Aryan race. Modern concerns regarding "designer babies" are an echo of much older concerns! A related, emerging problem lies in the potential political or economic uses to which increased genetic information might be put. One issue, already the subject of serious discussion, is the feasibility of predicting criminal or addictive personalities before birth. Knowledge about an individual's genetic make-up may also be used in the future by those who assess insurance risks or for other economic or employment calculations. As our knowledge and the technological possibilities at our disposal increase we ought to be concerned about the uses to which such genetic information may be put. In the near future this will pose many new moral and ethical dilemmas.

For the Christian the second category of concerns regarding the beliefs of this philosophy is even more disturbing. This is when genetic determinism is used to explain not only physical characteristics but also moral behaviours and orientations. Whilst there is no conclusive evidence that genes - alone and unaffected by other factors - determine our behavioural or sexual orientation, the belief that such genes must exist, only remaining to be discovered, is gaining increasing credence amongst opinion-formers in the West. If we were to accept that it is genetically pre-determined that we will behave in certain ways, morally and sexually, then this belief would have enormous implications for our understanding of biblical truth. It is already the case that many preachers and ministers, in their interpretation of Scriptures, are heavily influenced by this philosophy; or they simply choose to steer clear of certain subjects for fear of offending beliefs acquired through the media, in schools and so on.

In what ways does genetic determinism contradict or challenge traditional, orthodox Christian teaching with regards to morality and sexuality? In one respect, there is an apparent parallel. The Bible teaches that normal human behaviour is the result of the fallen nature of man, resulting in a life governed by dominant passions and thus a life of inevitable sin in the eyes of a righteous God. The effects of the Fall were physical and congenital, as well as moral and spiritual. This theological viewpoint could sound, at first, a bit like the inescapable outworking of our genetic construct but in genetic determinism there is no God, there is no eternal punishment (because there is no right or wrong), there is no Fall to explain our behaviour, and there is little or no possibility for change – unless it is by medical or surgical means.

There are other, equally obvious, differences. To say, for example, that certain sexual behaviour is "natural" is to contradict clearly stated Scriptures such as Romans 1:26-27, in which certain sexual behaviours are described as *"shameful"*, *"unnatural"* and subject to divine punishment. The word *"unnatural"* in Romans could be interpreted as not conforming to contemporary (Jewish) social norms, but this interpretation does not solve the problem for those who seek to marry genetic determinism with a belief in the Bible.

In 1 Corinthians 6:9-11 Paul makes three clear assertions: that certain behaviours are considered wicked and disqualify the person who commits them from God's Kingdom; secondly, that there is a tendency to deceive ourselves about these behaviours; and thirdly, some of the congregation at Corinth who were governed by these behaviours had since been transformed. It strikes me that this passage offers hope for those who wish to change, whereas there is a hopeless fatalism in genetic determinism, which argues that we are what we are and as such we must remain. If the latter were true, how is it that the people whom Paul knew in Corinth changed? It is worth noting that this transformation came about despite contemporary Greek social and moral beliefs. Corinth had a notorious reputation in the Classical World for an "anything goes" moral climate. It was like some cities in today's Western World: it took pride in shocking those whom it saw as holding outmoded, conservative moral viewpoints. To be accused of "Corinthianism" was to be classified as hopelessly corrupt and debauched. Thankfully for Corinthian converts the church had overseers and teachers, instructed by Paul, who offered the imperative and the hope of inner transformation through Christ.

Those who wish to embrace absolute genetic determinism must end up by questioning the validity of Scripture or, inspired by other philosophies, they may seek to "improve" upon Scripture in the light of modern thinking, knowledge and beliefs (just as the Corinthians were presumably tempted to do).

The challenge for Christian churches that wish to teach the Bible as literal truth is that, having identified certain behaviours as being unnatural and sinful in God's eyes, they must then surely offer a teaching and pastoral regime that welcomes and accepts any individual into the church whilst their problems are identified and helped, to the point where they can say, with Paul, "*Some of you were like that...*". Transformation is only possible because of the compassion and grace of God. It is a process of change, which combines divine grace with divine challenges. This process must begin, though, with a clear distinction drawn between right and wrong. The God kind of love, loves us too much to leave us as we are!

Humanism

Simply put, humanism is a belief that there is no god, neither is there any spiritual reality. It places man and the human mind at the centre of his own universe.

In a recent survey in England, roughly one third of those polled claimed to be humanists. Polls in European countries fluctuate and in North America the figure is not as high but it is clear that in the West humanism is a very popular and influential philosophy. Humanism, in its various forms, owes much to the Enlightenment and the growth of rationalism in the seventeenth and eighteenth centuries. However, it has ancient roots and has existed for many centuries. For example, the beliefs of early Greek philosophers such as Heraclitus and Protagoras sound very "modern" to the contemporary Western reader, believing as they did that, "Man is the measure of all things". Before the Enlightenment, in the sixteenth century, the French philosopher and playwright Rabelais expressed his version of humanism through his *thelemaic* philosophy, which stated that "whatever you wish to do you should do – that is the only real law". This sounds very like the core value of the "me" generation recently popularised in the West. This view, of man situated at the centre of his own universe, became increasingly influential in the late nineteenth century and during the twentieth century when humanism's twin belief – atheism – was at its height.

It is enormously appealing to follow Rabelais' lead, to encourage individuals to throw off all restraint and do only what they wish to do. This idea at first sounds very liberating but a moment's thought demonstrates how socially, as well as morally, bankrupt this philosophy is. What if I want to murder? Or steal? Or I'm a surgeon who decides he can't be bothered to operate on a given day? The philosophy is manifestly self-indulgent and completely impractical!

Humanism, in its various forms, gained a significant influence on European and North American thinking in the decades after the

Second World War. Britain, for example, became a post-Christian nation long before the advent of multi-culture, multi-faith and a multitude of moral issues that emerged to challenge the authority of the Christian church in the late twentieth century. Through a combination of humanism, liberalism, atheism and indecisive Christian leadership, church attendance plummeted during the decades between 1945 and 1975. The resultant weakness of the church left it poorly placed to speak with a strong, united voice. The Christian recovery only began with the charismatic and evangelical revivals of the 1970s and 1980s and is now being aided by an influx into Europe of African, Asian and North and South American Christians.

Contemporary humanists would contend that they have developed non-religious moral and ethical beliefs which are superior to Christianity, arguing that humanism can "unite" mankind in the face of religious divisions. This conclusion has led to a social experiment, which has been adopted by some European nations in an attempt to solve the problems created by multi-faith and increasingly ethnically diverse societies. For this social experiment to succeed, qualities such as "tolerance" became the priority as all faiths and cultures have to be esteemed as being of equal value. Many of the apologists for this brand of thinking are humanist; despising all religious faith, they find it easy to be "tolerant"! Such tolerance must, in practice, be intolerant of the exclusive claims of any single religion since exclusivity threatens to expose the cracks that are carefully papered over in such a society. The misguided jettisoning of our European Christian heritage by politicians eager to prove their credentials as tolerant secularists has led in several states to an increasing moral confusion. Given that all belief systems are ultimately exclusive in their claims (that is, each one claims to teach "the" truth) any attempt to create a multi-faith society based purely on an anodyne, secular tolerance that thinly disguises its contempt for all religious belief is doomed to failure. What succeeds historically is a national confidence in its own religious identity, coupled with freedom of religious observance, built upon the freedom of individual conscience – preferably free from political interference. Abandoning a nation's Christian heritage will only temporarily appease Christianity's enemies. In the meantime it will jeopardise the very values upon which such a society is built.

Another popular aspect of humanism can be found in a twentieth century trend: towards rationalism and away from religious explanations for "the big questions". In our modern, scientific world many people in the West uncritically accept a non-biblical explanation for the origin, purpose and destiny of mankind. The belief system of humanism would argue that only things and ideas that are demonstrable and comprehensible to human intellect may be accepted as the truth. According to this philosophy, truth is therefore a never-ending process of scientific discovery and proof. The enemy of reason – humanists and atheists would argue – is religious faith. According to the Bible:

"To have faith is to be sure of the things we hope for, to be certain of the things we cannot see." [18]

In Romans 10:5-17, we read that this faith comes from hearing the truth of God, as expressed in the Gospel. It is, therefore, a faith that is based on a revealed truth. This, to humanists, is superstitious nonsense. Instead, they will put their trust in whichever scientific theory is currently fashionable or which seems most pleasing.

There are two main attractions, as I see it, to the philosophy of humanism. Firstly, if there is no God, and therefore no ultimate judge of sin, then right and wrong – as moral absolutes – cease to matter as there are no eternal consequences for our actions. Secondly, if there is no God we can all be truly free to be masters of our own destinies. We become, as the serpent in Genesis would say, "like gods". For humanism positions the individual human being at the centre of his own subjective universe. As a teenager, before I became a Christian, I was once asked when I thought the world would end? I replied, "When I die." Of course this was youthful vanity but for the humanist there is no life after death, no eternal destiny. Subjectively, therefore – for the humanist – his or her world will indeed end when he or she dies.

The result of humanism, as outlined above, is to encourage a hedonism devoid of the fear of divine punishment or reward. Rabelais'

"Do what thou wilt" becomes the only meaningful law: do whatever you want to do. Polonius's advice, in *Hamlet*, "To thine own self be true" expresses a similar, popular sentiment. Humanism encourages all of this – a life of apparent individual freedom, without shame or guilt, where the only being you have to answer to is yourself. Put another way, it promotes a self-seeking, self-absorbed life that is careless of its impact on others. This life is very appealing to fallen human nature!

A growing set of ethical concerns is currently emerging in the West as the result of an increasing tendency amongst some scientific humanists to treat human beings as just another animal species. If man is merely another animal then this logically opens the door to, for instance, scientific research that combines human with animal eggs or sperm. The Bible portrays man as unique, distinct from the animal kingdom in many vital respects. Ironically humanism, in respect of scientific rationalism, reduces man to the level of just another biological species, different in kind but perhaps not in value to other animals.

In summary, the notion of individual improvement, for the humanist, lies in the full exploitation of each person's talents and energies to achieve personal success and happiness. More vaguely, humanists may simply wish to "live life to the full" (the definition or measure of "fulfilment" is always very personal to the individual but is generally expressed in terms of the selfish pursuit of "happiness" – as if selfishness ever made anyone happy!). Humanism will argue that the answers to our problems always lie within; our nature is not fallen, they will argue, it is fundamentally good and full of hidden possibilities.

Most "self help" books have, as their philosophical basis, a form of humanism. In this respect, humanism is diametrically opposed to the Bible's analysis of human nature. Humanism also downplays spirituality – it tends to exist in a purely material, psychological, cognitive and emotional universe – so that spiritual re-birth leading to a relationship with a spiritual God is not credible and therefore not desirable. One of Satan's most powerful temptations, presented to Adam and Eve in Genesis 3:5, was that – if they ate the forbidden fruit – they would become "like God" (or, "like gods"). Humanism perpetuates this delusion.

Mockery

Mockery is not a philosophy, nor even necessarily a coherent set of ideas. It constitutes an attitude of sneering superiority, which may be based upon a set of values or beliefs hostile to Christianity; or it may be based on more vague feelings of animosity or prejudice that would tend to write Christianity off as being ridiculous in some way. I only include it here because mockery is a very powerful weapon in the hands of Christianity's enemies. It has caused much doubt, dismay and unbelief amongst Christians over the centuries. I also include it because – however superficial it is in its understanding – it is often rooted in one or more of the "big, dangerous" ideas explored in this chapter.

One example of subtle mockery – almost negative scepticism – in the Bible, is provided by Job's "comforters". You may view Zophar, Bildad and Eliphaz as being merely misguided but, basically, well-meaning friends of Job's – or you may detect a consistently mocking tone in most of what they say. There is no mistaking Eliphaz's attitude of superiority, when he says, for example:

> " 'Empty words, Job! Empty words! No wise person
> would talk as you do…' " [19]

What is indisputable is that the effect of their words must have been deeply discouraging and potentially damaging to Job's faith in God, during a dreadful test. In a test you find out who your true friends are!

A more obvious example of mockery, used as a direct attack on the faith of a man of God, can be found in the story of Nehemiah, and his extraordinary venture to rebuild the walls of Jerusalem. This was a project that required great faith, unity of purpose and determination. Sanballat and Tobiah voiced their contempt for the plan very openly:

> "When Sanballat heard that we the Jews had
> begun rebuilding the wall, he was furious and

began to ridicule us. In front of his companions and the Samaritan troops he said, 'What do these miserable Jews think they're doing? Do they intend to rebuild the city? Do they think that by offering sacrifices they can finish the work in one day? Can they make building stones out of heaps of burnt rubble?' Tobiah was standing there beside him, and he added, 'What kind of wall could they ever build? Even a fox could knock it down!' "[20]

Do the words of this Satanic double act sound familiar? Look at the elements of their mockery: they expressed forceful contempt to an audience of critics, waverers and doubters; they made personal and racial insults; they expressed scorn for the vision of Nehemiah; they cast doubt on God's word and character; they sneered at Nehemiah's resources; they were contemptuous of the Jews' abilities; they ridiculed the value and durability of what the Jews were doing. Look at Nehemiah's response to this mockery. In Chapter 4:4, Nehemiah's reaction is to take the situation to God, immediately, (rather than brood upon the discouragement). They continued with the work, with increased security, and in Chapter 6:1ff Nehemiah discerns their trickery and calls upon God for strength. He lets the power of God do his talking for him. He offers firm, consistent leadership and, by Chapter 6:15, the wall was finished – in fifty-two days!

Christ was subject to much severe mockery before His crucifixion. Satan used this ancient, powerful weapon against our Lord in a vain attempt to discourage Him from fulfilling His Father's will. In Luke 23:11 for example, it states that, *"Herod and his soldiers mocked Jesus…"*.

Mockery is particularly effective against those who fear man, or whose faith has been weakened. Before I became a Christian I, like many, assumed that Christianity was for weak-willed souls who (bless them) didn't know any better! My attitude was, to my shame, one of ignorant superiority often expressed mockingly, in word and tone. When faced with mockery, we should quietly forgive and pray for the mocker, ask God for strength for ourselves, continue with our divine calling and continue to hold fast to our faith because that is the very thing that mockery is intended to undermine. If the wall of our faith is built on strong foundations then the "little foxes" sent by Satan to jump against it will never cause it to fall.

Moral Liberalism

Moral Liberalism is not one single, coherent philosophy – rather, it is more accurately defined as a set of values and attitudes. "Liberal" is often used as an adjective before another "ism", for example, "liberal humanism". Some definitions and many applications of the word "liberal" are very positive. To be a liberal person is to be generous, concerned and kind; and to live in a liberal democracy means that most citizens enjoy many benefits. But the word "liberal" also feeds into twentieth and twenty-first century thinking in other, more negative ways. At heart liberalism is a belief in notions of personal liberty. In a secularised society this concept of freedom does not take the Bible as its measure of right and wrong behaviour; rather, concepts of freedom are based on humanist principles of personal and social choices, tolerance and happiness. The potential dangers associated with this philosophy are expressed in the more negative uses of the word, such as the old-fashioned word "libertine", which refers to someone who exploits notions of personal freedom to lead an immoral or selfish life.

Liberalism tends to view authority structures and figures as suspect. It will tend to accept that bad people will do bad things but woe betide the police, the judiciary or the government if they make a genuine mistake! The Apostle Paul lived under the rule of Roman government, which was famously efficient but brutally repressive. This government would eventually execute him as the result of spurious charges. Yet if you read the Thirteenth Chapter of Romans, you will not find him encouraging a liberal or anti-authoritarian view of government. Paul does not advocate agreement with everything any government does or says, but neither does he encourage constant carping against authority. Liberalism views governments and authority as potentially, or actually, the enemies of personal freedom: Romans 13 describes governments as gifts from God, to order and safeguard otherwise anarchic, chaotic societies. To question and challenge governments is healthy and desirable: such criticism is made impossible in tyrannies. But Western cynicism has become corrosive. In a democracy we have responsibilities as well as rights. Many in the West are now concerned that the balance between rights and responsibilities has become harmfully distorted. There is also the concern that constant criticism of government may weaken the very fabric of democratic societies. It is undeniable that a Christian Democracy will have a healthy regard for a biblical view of liberty: it is when liberalism becomes hostile to biblical teaching that we must see it, as practising Christians, as potentially harmful.

It is in its view of personal morality that liberalism differs most from biblical teaching. Because of its suspicion of over-legislation – as a means by which a government may enforce its will upon individual citizens – secular forms of moral liberalism will tend to oppose most laws concerning personal morality. To defend this viewpoint, liberalism finds it necessary to argue a fundamental idea: that morality is ultimately an individual set of personal choices which, provided they are not harmful to anyone else, are the business only of that individual. The Bible is viewed by liberals as outmoded, conservative and irrelevant. Moral liberalism would argue that no one else has the right to question an individual's private moral choices and bents. Surely, they would argue, if there is a "loving" God then He would always sympathise with, and even condone these choices? The New Testament, however, teaches us that mankind's freedom of choice is an illusion. Rather than being free, each man or woman is, in fact, controlled by inner passions and desires:

> *"Actually all of us [Christians] were like them [people who disobey God] and lived according to our natural desires, doing whatever suited the wishes of our own bodies and minds..."* [21]

The Bible teaches us that these passions and desires have always produced a form of slavery – not freedom – slavery to sin:

> *"Surely you know that when you surrender yourselves as slaves to obey someone, you are in fact the slaves of the master you obey – either of sin, which results in death, or of obedience, which results in being put right with God".* [22]

As we also see in this verse, there are consequences - including divine punishment – for our deeds.

Moral Liberalism is much more interested in causes than in their consequences. It does not approve of New Testament notions of absolute standards of moral behaviour, nor of divine judgement. Liberalism tends to accept the popular moral status quo, and agonises over psychological, social, political or economic causes when truly awful things happen. Conversely, Christianity exposes the need for, and offers the hope of, individual and social transformation.

As a result of this emphasis on moral freedom and the rights of individuals, moral liberalism has cultivated an individualism that has contributed to the breakdown of the traditional nuclear family and, therefore, of social cohesion. There are those who argue for a more liberal view of what constitutes God's ideal of the "family" but I cannot, in all conscience, see a clear scriptural mandate for anything other than the traditional nuclear family. All relevant secular research demonstrates the desirability for children to have the care of a father and a mother. That is not to say that single parent families cannot be successful, neither is it to say that some marriages are not harmful. However, hard cases make poor spiritual laws and we ignore God's plans at our peril. If I am free to choose, and put my own happiness first, then my commitment to others will often be weakened. For example, instead of marrying I will seek to obtain all the benefits of marriage without its responsibilities. If I am free to choose I will tend to subordinate the needs of others to my own desires. The cult of individualism has increased in the West since the 1950s and it could be argued that this over-emphasis on individualism has led to a breakdown in social structures, responsibilities, authority and cohesion.

As a consequence of the current importance given to the notion of moral "tolerance" it has become increasingly difficult to characterise any human behaviour as "wrong, "immoral" or "sinful". The Bible also has much to say about tolerance and inclusion; it was - especially for the period when the New Testament was written – very radical in its views about women, slavery, social class and race. However, where liberal views of tolerance and biblical grace part company is in the set of assertions by a Holy God that certain behaviours are righteous whereas other human behaviours are unacceptable. In much of the West today, few politicians dare to mention moral solutions to moral problems, for fear of being branded "intolerant". There is also pressure on churches to avoid words like "sin" for fear of sounding intolerant.

Therefore, moral liberalism has had a huge impact on popular moral opinion and even on modern theology. It has also encouraged a radical questioning of the authority of the church, of the Bible and even of God Himself. This is not the place for a detailed study of Liberal Theology (a diverse and complex movement, tracing its roots back to the Enlightenment) but, suffice to say, its results have been catastrophic for church attendance in some Western nations that were once predominantly Christian. By contrast, Third World Evangelical Christianity, which is rooted in the certainties of nineteenth century revivals and their resultant missionary service, looks on in amazement and dismay at the uncertainty and unbelief expressed by some Western academics, theologians and church leaders. At the height of the popularity of the Liberal Theology movement, Dr. Robinson, Bishop of Woolwich, in his book *Honest to God*, questioned the very existence of God as a distinct omnipotent Being. To many in his camp, God was dead! How, I wonder, can anyone work with integrity for someone who does not exist? And why should we expect anyone to attend church each Sunday to listen to someone else's doubts and unbelief (honestly held as these may be)? Doubt and unbelief were the inevitable consequences of viewing the Bible as a book like any other – susceptible to denial and disapproval where it appears "outdated", "wrong" or "irrelevant". Unless the Bible is viewed as inspired, infallible and eternally true then each individual is left free to develop a personal syncretism – a mixture of the personally pleasing elements of the Bible with elements of more "modern" thinking about the human condition. This syncretism is designed to validate the moral and ethical framework that is most appealing to the individual at that particular time. In this way we change the Bible, rather than the Bible changing us. Freedom of moral choice without any external constraint, such as the Bible, lies at the heart of liberalism. There are few philosophies in this chapter that are less tolerant of the exclusive claims of biblical Christianity than moral liberalism.

Nationalism

Extreme forms of Nationalism are expressed in terms of adulation for one's state or ethnic group, the superiority of which is unquestioned. More wars have been fought for the cause of nationalism than for religion, though these causes are sometimes confused. Nationalism appears to be a purely political philosophy but when we read the Book of Daniel in the Bible we see the spiritual forces at work behind aggressive nationalism. There is absolutely nothing wrong, and a great deal that is right, with loving your native country and wishing it to be blessed by God. However, I believe that very negative aspects of nationalism will soon emerge in the West (and further afield), potentially causing much secular conflict and even division within the Church of Jesus Christ. In part, this upsurge of nationalism will come as a reaction against globalisation, mass migration and the creation of supra-national trading blocs and communities.

Economic crises have also traditionally fuelled nationalism – which feeds on a mixture of fear and pride. Nationalism will articulate the fears of certain ethnic groups that feel under threat in nations in which demographics are rapidly changing due to migrations of various peoples, or which have a sizeable minority population that is historic but distinctive. Extreme forms of nationalism will also be promoted by ethnic groups that contain individuals who feel innately superior to others, but who also feel that their identity is under threat.

Social Darwinism is a controversial extension of Darwinian theory, which portrays ethnic, social or national groups as constantly competing, rather than collaborating, so that "survival of the fittest" is a term and ethic that can be applied to racial or social groupings as well as to animal species. Those who advocate it may implicitly or explicitly fuel a notion of national or racial superiority. In some Western countries this process may also be accelerated by the possible failure of secular attempts at social unity and attempts to create a coherent, heterogeneous national identity, within a multi-faith context. All of this will be intensified by demonic hatred and fear.

With the disintegration of various European Empires during the hundred years from 1850 to 1950 the Nation State became enormously important as a tangible expression of individual, cultural, linguistic and social identity. Nations are still coming into being, as new or ancient expressions of ethnic identities and aspirations continue to redefine borders in most continents. In Africa this process is particularly fluid, especially in regions where identification with the tribe is stronger than it is with the nation.

The new, twenty-first century "empires" are conglomerates of trading nation states, such as the European Union. These inevitably tend towards centralisation, leaving ethnic groups feeling marginalised, disenfranchised and vulnerable. The resulting populist trend, during the next fifty years, back to a resurgence of "grass-roots" nationalism, will create enormous international and intra-national tensions and may even lead to open conflict, especially as natural resources begin to run out and as populations increase.

These issues will pose challenges for the Christian Church, for several reasons. Firstly, politics and faith have seldom mixed happily. Secondly, there will be regions where conflict slows or prevents evangelism. Thirdly, the church will increasingly be faced with the challenge to marry the eternal gospel with a volatile contemporary political scene. And, fourthly, inter-church cooperation and unity will have to improve to set an example of unity and compassion in a conflicted, frightened world. The church, as well as individuals, will be transformed in this fiery furnace.

I believe, also, that nationalism will appear to some to be a reasonable response to concerns within Western societies which are seen to be growing more and more unstable. An historic example of this occurred in Germany in the 1920s and 1930s, where hope was increasingly pinned on the rabidly nationalistic Nazis, as opposed to the old, political guard who inherited a post First World War peace settlement that humiliated and crippled Germany. A heady mix of national economic uncertainty, ethical breakdown and social and political uncertainty always has the potential to lead to extreme, right (or left) wing solutions. Religious freedom and tolerance under such governments is always problematic. Religious persecution could well occur directly and also peripherally, as the values and mission of the church – which transcend national boundaries – come into conflict with more extreme forms of nationalism.

New Age

The set of beliefs we often refer to as New Age has been thoroughly discussed and documented by others. Some commentators have rightly said that much of "New Age" is really "Old Paganism" as it frequently takes for its diverse spiritual teachings pre- or extra- Christian spiritual sources. These teachings often have their roots in regional expressions of paganism or in older, Eastern religions. Where New Age borrows heavily from Eastern mysticism and religions, it does so mainly to inform many aspects of alternative medicine and therapies. In some ways New Age is also close to spiritualism and the occult in its interpretation of man's spiritual relationship with Nature.

New Age helped to fill a contemporary spiritual void in modern Western societies, a void brought about in the second half of the twentieth century by increasing secularism and by forms of theology that deny or down-play genuine Christian spiritual experience. Moreover, New Age – like the occult and unlike Christianity – avoids moral teaching and judgements. New Age claims to bring healing and personality changes through a host of psychic and physical treatments and therapies that are so popular that any High Street in Britain will display evidence of their appeal. The scientific rationalist laughs all of this off as quackery but struggles to explain its popularity without resorting to condescension.

Some Christians may view New Age as harmless, however, the practising Christian needs to be very wary of any kind of "treatment" or "cure" linked with a spiritual belief system that lies outside the Bible as these generally have their roots in paganism or Eastern mysticism. This spiritual health warning includes many alternative medicines and therapies, spiritual relaxation regimes, some other popular healing approaches widely on offer today, and also the spiritual teaching associated with advanced stages of certain martial arts.

Aspects of New Age are also attractive to certain movements in Christianity, finding their way directly or indirectly into unorthodox Christian mysticism. The serious Christian disciple must be very careful of any method, language or instruction which lies outside clear biblical teaching and is closer to New Age practices than to biblical Christianity. The spiritual experiences offered by these New Age methods will appear to bring joy through access to spiritual "reality" but will ultimately deceive and damage the unwary.

Occultism

Of all of the "big, dangerous" ideas in this chapter, few are as seductive as the occult, to the human spirit. We have already seen that man is a tripartite being, consisting of body, soul and spirit. Various appeals are made by other "big, dangerous ideas" to material man, to his body, his mind and to his emotions. Occultism, in its various forms, offers to fill the spiritual void into which man was cast by his Fall. We can see this seductive power at work in the West, with the consistent re-emergence of witchcraft in children's and adult fiction, and in all forms of the media. During a conversation I had with an African Christian at a large conference, she expressed astonishment that witchcraft is considered as so much harmless fun in Western Literature. Coming from Africa she knew it to be anything but harmless fun! Almost an entire generation in the West is being brought up in ignorance of the Bible but they are being fed on a spiritual diet of witchcraft, masquerading as harmless fantasy. Someone once said that the devil's greatest trick is to deceive people into thinking he does not exist.

Like New Age and Pseudo-Christian Cults the various branches of occultism recognise man as an actual or potential spiritual being. Each individual, occultism would argue, has a spiritual dimension longing to contact a spiritual reality outside herself or himself. Many of the "big, dangerous" ideas, examined in this chapter, lead man away from spirituality and therefore away from God. The occult creates false paths that mislead man into devotion to false gods. The Bible identifies the occult as being powerfully deceptive and clearly states that it must be shunned by those who love God.

We are taught in the Bible that there are two main categories of occult activity or practice: divination and sorcery. Divination would claim to be the acquisition of knowledge through spiritual means, such as fortune-telling, ESP and various psychic methods – this knowledge being made comprehensible to the human mind by an external spiritual force or personality. One of the clearest examples of divination in the New Testament is the story of the slave girl in Acts 16:16-22. Sorcery invades or seeks to control physical senses, people or objects; its means of doing so include drugs, potions, charms, incantations and so on. These are merely the channels through which spiritual forces operate. Sorcery is included in a list of heinous, unrepented activities in Revelation 9:20-21 (along with murder, theft and sexual immorality).

How does God view occultism? The Bible makes it very clear:

> *"Don't sacrifice your children in the fires on your altars; and don't let your people practise divination or look for omens or use spells or charms, and don't let them consult the spirits of the dead. The Lord your God hates people who do these disgusting things..."* [23]

God *hates* occultism (the word for *"hates"* is a Hebrew word that expresses the strength of God's loathing). God finds the occult disgusting, and He punishes it. Now, most people in the West would say, "Of course I wouldn't sacrifice a child in a fire!" But God also says we are not to *"look for omens"*. How many read "the stars"? Or consult a fortune-teller? And mediums and psychics still claim to contact the dead on behalf of their paying clients.

Where there is no strong Christian presentation of the Gospel of Christ, the unwary will flock to fortune-tellers, mediums and psychics to satisfy their innate spiritual hunger.

Pantheism

This is a very ancient idea with some modern manifestations. Put simply, pantheism is the belief that god is in all things, circumscribed by creation. This belief is common to those who love nature to the point of worship, and it is also similar to some aspects of some Eastern religions (for example, there are resonances of pantheism in Hinduism though the latter has retained its ancient belief in many, self-existent gods).

Pantheism dismisses any idea of an all-powerful Creator who exists outside of creation. It rejects biblical teachings about the after-life, judgement and resurrection. According to pantheism, after death the individual is re-absorbed into creation as every living thing is believed to possess equal spiritual worth. The idea that man is uniquely made in the image of God, and the biblical imperative of the need for individual change, is alien to pantheism, which stresses the need to attune individual sensitivity and imagination to the natural world around us. The greatest difference between pantheism and Christian beliefs, lies in the concept of a Creator God separate from and superior to His creation. We are specifically commanded in the Bible not to worship creation, or anything made with human hands.

A primitive form of pantheism is "animism". This is the worship of animals or other aspects of nature, sometimes involving witchcraft and the alleged ability of humans to be able to take on or borrow the qualities of some animals. Throughout the Americas, Asia and Africa especially, different forms of animism were (or are) very dominant within some indigenous cultures. In the West, this belief system sometimes finds expression through the popular media when fictional characters experience metamorphosis and are changed into another creature.

Pseudo-Christian Cults

There are many religions around the world today that completely deny the authenticity of the Bible: their god (or gods) and their holy writ are peculiar to them. It is relatively easy to distinguish them from orthodox Christianity. However, there are also pseudo-Christian groups that claim as theirs the true heritage of Jewish or Christian roots. They also claim a superior revelation to that of Orthodox Christianity. This "superior" revelation often came through one man or woman but was then built upon by others (often resulting in schisms within these movements) to construct an alternative view of God, of Jesus our Saviour, and of His relationship with man. At first sight, or on first hearing, many of these religious systems can seem very similar to orthodox Christianity in their teaching (some such movements, for example, use "God", or even "Christ" in their titles). The Christian must be wary of these pathways, which may *seem* like the truth but which, on closer inspection, clearly deviate significantly from it.

There are too many such pseudo-Judaic or pseudo-Christian movements to name here but they all tend to have one or more of three core heresies in common. The first concerns the person and status of Jesus Christ. Orthodox Christians (see, for example, the Statement of Faith of the Evangelical Alliance) believe Christ to be the Second Person of the Trinity – fully divine and fully human – He is Lord, Saviour, Baptiser and Coming King (for many He is also Healer, and so much more.). We see Him honoured in the Bible from Genesis to Revelation. The greatest theological battle fought through apologetics by the Early Church Fathers, in the post-Apostolic period, was with those who denied the divinity or the humanity of Christ. This will be one of the greatest areas of attack by the spirit of anti-Christ in the last days. Be very wary of any teaching that devalues or undermines Christ – it will always be a deception, spawned by the devil.

Secondly, in most of these cults belief in eternal judgement is watered down or denied – most of them will teach that there is no hell, no place of eternal punishment.

Thirdly, the Bible makes it clear in its final book that it offers a completed written revelation of God's will:

> *"I, John, solemnly warn everyone who hears the prophetic words of this book: if anyone adds anything to them, God will add to his or her punishment the plagues described in this book. And if anyone takes anything away from the prophetic words of this book, God will take away from them their share of the fruit of the tree of life and of the Holy City, which are described in this book."* [24]

This quotation refers specifically, of course, to the Book of Revelation but the canon of Scripture as a whole is entirely completed, unique and authoritative. Despite this, cults will claim that their own commentaries, "translations" or "inspired" texts are equally authoritative, or even superior to, the Bible. Like the Gnostic heretics of the Early Church period they generally argue that these texts or commentaries teach a "higher truth" – revealed only to the privileged few. The Bible warns us of false prophets [25] and false teachers:

> *"False prophets appeared in the past among the people, and in the same way false teachers will appear among you. They will bring in destructive, untrue doctrines, and will deny the Master who redeemed them, and so they will bring upon themselves sudden destruction."* [26]

and even false Messiahs:

> *"For false Messiahs and false prophets will appear; they will perform great miracles and wonders*

*in order to deceive even God's chosen people, if
possible"* [27]

As we approach the end of this age, Satan will "throw everything"
he can at the Christian Church, in order to deceive and mislead as many
as possible. The broad and easy pathway of deception and delusion will
be crowded. But Jesus, who is *the* Way, will return to expose, confound
and judge all that is false.

These are all problems as old as Christianity itself. The story of
Simon Magus in Acts 8:9-24 offers an early example of the powerful
enticement provided by false cults. Simon, a Samaritan, offered money
to the apostles for spiritual power (hence the term *simony*). Having
been rebuked by Peter, Simon continued to establish his own cult,
built around himself. He claimed to be the incarnate God who came
to earth, in part to rescue a slave-prostitute of Tyre (Helene, with whom
he travelled and taught). He established a very popular, early Gnostic
cult in Rome, which attracted a large following and which influenced
many (there may even have been a statue erected in his honour by
Claudius Caesar). Simon rejected the Old Testament and claimed to
embody a "pure" form of Christianity that was superior to the teaching
of the Apostles. A number of Early Church Fathers, such as Irenaeus
(in *Against Heresies*) wrote to warn Christians of the enticements offered
by false teachers such as Simon. A thumbnail sketch of the beliefs of
founders of cults often sounds ridiculous but we must not underestimate
the magnetism exerted by false prophets and teachers.

Near the end of the Epistle to the Romans, Paul gives us an insight
into the nature of the appeal of the false teachers who were already
infiltrating the Early Church at the time when he wrote this letter. In
Chapter 16:17-19 Paul commends the Christians in Rome for their
loyalty and obedience but he also says that these qualities are not
enough. Christians need to add to these qualities the wisdom that
comes from being *"well versed and wise as to what is good"* (v.19 AB).
The Bible repeatedly states that the best way to recognise the false is to
have a very good knowledge of the true. If someone is trained to identify
genuine bank notes he will always spot the counterfeit. We do not need

to know the teaching of every cult and heresy – if we know the Word of God well, and have the Holy Spirit as our guide, then we will discern the false very quickly.

Paul warns that the false can be very enticing. The false teacher, he says in verse 18, is motivated by a voracious appetite for gain, power or celebrity; the teachers of the false are driven as well as convincing – they seek to fill the emptiness of their lives with ministry success, finance and fame. Paul also exposes their techniques: they use "ingratiating" and flattering speech to win over the listener; they are very gifted showmen and communicators. The effect of their smooth-talking teaching is very damaging, they *"create dissensions and difficulties, in opposition to the doctrine – the teaching – which you have been taught"* (v.17, AB).

In verses 25-26 Paul gives the antidote to this appealing fools' gold: it is for each individual Christian to know the revelation of the truth of the Gospel, taught clearly in the Word of God. This Gospel has been revealed in signs as well as by words, in the incarnation, life, ministry, crucifixion, resurrection and ascension of Christ. The Gospel also faithfully casts light on all the (Old Testament) prophetic Scriptures.

A key biblical warning is expressed by significant contributors to the New Testament: Paul (Galatians 1:8), Jude (10-20), Peter (2 Peter 2:8-22) and John (2 John 10) all warn us to have nothing to do with what is false. Let us heed the wisdom of these apostles and, like the Bereans, test all that we hear against the Word of God.

By the end of this age – before the return of Christ – the Bible predicts that a powerful, false, global religion will arise. It will be plausible and it will be apparently "legitimised" by accompanying signs and wonders. It will support the political power of an evil World Leader and work in harness with him to dominate mankind and direct worship away from the true God. One of the objectives of the spirit of antichrist (who will be behind this religion) will be to deceive "the elect", if that were possible. Satan has always sought worship, and in that sense Christ is his triumphant rival[28].

An interesting insight into the ultimate plans of Satan is offered by a study of the temptations of Christ[29]. In his third and greatest temptation of Christ, Satan offers Jesus rule over the *"kingdoms of the world"*.

Notice that Jesus does not contradict Satan's authority to make this offer – Satan is called *"the god of this world"* in 2 Corinthians 4:4. This offer is made on condition that Jesus should *"kneel down and worship me [Satan]"*. This is a temptation that the apparently messianic Man of Sin[30] will not be able to resist. Satan's aim is not merely to deceive man into failing to worship God, it is to direct this worship towards himself. For man has been made to worship something or someone!

Psychologism

By "psychologism" I mean the philosophy, or understanding of human nature, that underpins most branches of non-Christian psychology and psychiatry. This philosophy portrays all individuals as essentially, or potentially, good. It believes that our current human frailties and shortcomings are generally the result of what has happened to us in the past; experiences that have led to unresolved inner conflicts. Psychologism has had an enormous and subtle influence on the Christian Church in the West, with the resultant increase in the cult of individualism.

There are too many sources and branches of self-help, psychology, psychiatry and counselling to mention here. With the growth of the world-wide web there are many sites dedicated to the promotion of courses and therapies, which all claim to transform the individual through self-help, positive-thinking and other psychological techniques. Their titles vary but they will typically be called New Life Course, Renewing the Mind, Personal Transitional Techniques and so on. With the growth in the West of rationalist, scientifically based apparent solutions to all of our ills, these approaches and techniques have become very popular. In an age of increasing individual alienation and the breakdown of traditional families and societies, counselling offers friendship and listening, caring attentiveness: at a price.

According to this philosophy (if we can call psychologism a philosophy), put simply, each individual is seen as a victim of what has happened to him (especially in childhood) and if only the damage caused by these events might be eradicated then the individual's true self will be free to blossom and develop. Whatever psychiatric or psychological approach is taken, moral judgements about this true, or "inner" self are - for the most part – carefully avoided and the individual is largely free to choose her or his own version of right and wrong. When healed from the past, psychologism argues, the individual will be able to pursue her or his own destiny, free from hurts, fears, guilt, obsessions and so on.

Religious faith is often portrayed in secular psychologism as being restrictive or even delusional. In describing psychologism as a "big, dangerous idea" I do not wish to be understood to be critical of all psychiatric practices or of Christian-based counselling. When approached from a Christian perspective, therapy and counselling can be very helpful. However, when therapy replaces repentance, or attempts are made to "improve" rather than "crucify" fallen human nature, then psychologism finds itself in direct opposition to biblical explanations of the human condition. This in turn leads to very different ideas about how individuals can be helped to change.

Psychologism offers a fundamentally different understanding of human nature from that of the Bible and it seeks to re-define "good" and "bad", or even to see such descriptions as irrelevant or unhelpful. In what key respects does psychologism tend to differ from orthodox Christian teaching?

- Firstly, psychologism tends to place the individual at the centre of her or his universe; God is either dispensed with altogether, or placed at the periphery of this subjective vision of reality.

- Secondly, most branches of psychologism take "as read" an atheistic, and evolutionary view of nature, humanity and of the nature of change. If God is believed not to exist it is therefore irrational and even potentially dangerous for the individual to believe in Him and to expect Him to intervene in the individual's process of transformation.

- Thirdly, there is a tendency to view the person being counselled as the victim of bad experiences, perpetrated by others (which is sometimes true), therefore they tend to be treated as being entirely innocent of responsibility for their actions. In this meta-narrative (explanation) of the human condition, individuals need a therapist – not a Saviour. This approach may result in some need for forgiveness but seldom, if ever, results in repentance.

- Fourthly, psychologism is much less radical than Christianity – the former seeks to improve rather than transform human nature.

- Fifthly, moral judgements are seen as enemies of diagnosis by the practitioners of psychologism; everything is reduced to an existential set of facts, in which "right" or "wrong" are viewed as unhelpful ideas.

Psychologism sounds very modern and appealing. For example, it is much more attractive to be portrayed as a "victim" than a "sinner". It is much easier to focus on the hurt done to us rather than that which we have inflicted on others. In one large Christian conference I asked the audience which of them had been hurt by someone else? Every hand went up. I then asked who had hurt someone else? About five hands went up! Someone out there is hurting an awful lot of people!

Even leading secular psychologists and psychiatrists would admit to limitations and failures in their approaches (contrast, for example, the success rates of Christian groups – such as Teen Challenge, or Jackie Pullinger's St Stephen's Society in Hong Kong – with secular treatments for similar powerful addiction problems). I believe this relative failure is because psychologism is based upon a false premise – it leaves God out of the picture. After all, if He created us is He not best placed to make us whole, according to His definition of what constitutes wholeness?

Relativism

This is one of the oldest and most appealing of the ideas to be considered in this chapter. It is much older than its most obvious source - seventeenth and eighteenth century rationalism - but it gained new momentum in the twentieth century with the spread of secularism in Western cultures. Relativism has influenced most of the other philosophies discussed in this chapter and is perhaps closest to natural human thought and inclinations. It is, therefore, a particularly potent "big, dangerous idea". We are all instinctive and practised social negotiators, and we often bring to God and His commandments this very human attitude and set of negotiating skills. But how appropriate is it to negotiate with God concerning His absolute truths and instructions?

Relativism argues that absolute truth does not exist, that we each develop a moral code and an understanding of life that we apply variously to complex situations as we experience them. For example, the straightforward but absolute biblical commandment, *"Thou shalt not kill"* becomes weakened through many qualifications. Relativism might argue that *"Thou shalt not kill"* is generally appropriate but will add an "unless" or "except". It is generally wrong to kill, it will argue, unless someone near and dear is endangered – or you and your community are under attack. When an absolute, divine directive becomes applied to the messy reality of life our first instinct is to negotiate it away, or qualify a general rule with many plausible exceptions. Pastoral situations in churches necessarily have to deal with these situations all the time, by seeking to apply biblical teachings to the complications of life. It does have to be said, in all fairness, that we apply absolute biblical truths as honestly as we can to the complexities of our lives. This challenge is different from arguing with God about what we know to be true.

The concept of a "Just War" is one example of this process of qualification. The idea of a "Just" (morally, theologically and legally defensible) War can be argued from the Old Testament examples of Israel's dealings with the inhabitants of the Promised Land. In the early Christian church the idea of Just War was first popularised by Augustine in *Civitas Dei* in the early fifth century and was codified in the thirteenth century by Thomas Aquinas. To defend warfare on moral and theological grounds has always required much intellectual dexterity! To kill large numbers of fellow human beings would, at first sight, clearly contravene the simple commandment, *"Thou shalt not kill"*;

but war has – at various times – seemed necessary or even desirable to Christian leaders or states, especially since the conversion of the Roman Emperor Constantine made Christianity a "state" religion. This has often required a fundamental re-interpretation of Scriptures – often employing Old Testament examples - in order to legitimise war.

In contrast, the New Testament takes the Old Testament commandment, *"Thou shalt not kill"* and – far from weakening it – strengthens it and turns a negative statement into a positive one. The general instruction of Paul:

> *"Love does no wrong to a neighbour; therefore love
> is the fulfilling of the Law"* [31]

reminds us of the extraordinary challenge made by Christ during the Sermon on The Mount:

> *"You have heard that it was said to men of old,
> Thou shalt not kill; and whoever kills shall be
> liable to judgement. But I say to you that every
> one who is angry with his brother shall be liable
> to judgement"* [32]

The New Testament teaches that *motives*, not just *actions*, should be pure and that the Christian should be inspired by love. Furthermore, we are to bless our enemies and those who wrong us[33] not curse them. Something very radical is being commanded here: no matter how counter intuitive it seems. As our hearts are changed by God, so are our motives and then our deeds. True Christianity should change us from the inside out, as it were, and sets standards of behaviour impossible to achieve without divine help. If we think of part of the famous Lord's Prayer[34] *"Thy will be done, on earth, as it is in heaven"*, we must surely acknowledge that this is another commandment that can only be achieved through divine help working on sanctified, submissive hearts that fully embrace God's manifesto of grace, love and forgiveness. We find this very difficult, for *"wide is the way and easy"* that leads to destruction. It is *easier* to hate our enemy than to forgive him: maybe even easier to kill him than love him? Obedience to God's commands is so challenging because it requires fundamental changes in us. The natural man is incapable of this level of grace, love and forgiveness so he will always excuse his reasons for disobeying divine commandments on the spurious grounds of pragmatism.

Of course, scriptural teaching always has to be applied to complex human conditions. This is never simple but it will always be aided by measuring what we think, feel and do against the absolute truth of scripture, revealed by the Holy Spirit. This is the true "mirror" we must hold up to ourselves. Relativism subtly erodes the sovereignty of God by reducing absolute truths to mere debating or negotiating points. I think we have all indulged in this at some time in our Christian lives! Think again of the verse quoted above from the Lord's prayer: *"Thy will be done on earth as it is in heaven"* (that is, with the same attitude of obedience God would see in heaven). Can you imagine an angel saying to God, in heaven, "Lord, are you sure about that?" Besides, relativism, by its very nature, is utterly inconsistent – initially attractive it proves, ultimately, to be shifting sand upon which to build. It moves, for example, from the near-absolutism of "it is never right – though sometimes understandable – to commit adultery", to the absolute relativism of, "thou shalt not steal – except from large companies or tax inspectors". It offers a DIY approach to morality and ethics. Most human beings are very bad at DIY!

As I have said, relativism has influenced much Christian thinking – especially in hermeneutics (the interpretation and teaching of the Bible) - sometimes to the point where the Bible itself is no longer accepted as God's infallible and inspired Word. It has also profoundly affected the secular world around us. At a personal, social or national level we often subjectively, or collectively, decide when and how to apply general biblical or legal requirements.

Secular manifestations of relativism offer interesting insights into the pervasiveness of this philosophy, as they affect the world around us every day. Recent polls in Britain, for example, indicate a growing number of citizens willing to defraud the tax system or lie or steal at work because this behaviour is rationalised as not being *real* dishonesty. Relativism portrays God as expressing opinions, not truths or commands, thus leaving modern Western society without any fixed star to steer by. Tempting as it is, relativism will ultimately prove to be utterly futile and unsatisfying, inevitably leading to a compromised set of values and an unfulfilled life.

Conclusions

Each of the philosophies considered in this chapter offers, in some form, an alternative view of the human condition to that which is taught in the Bible. Some of these philosophies have much academic literature devoted to them, some have shaped social institutions of all kinds, still others exist mainly in the popular consciousness and are expressed through the media of Western societies. What they have in common is that they are highly persuasive and influential and are, therefore, "big". They are also "dangerous" in the sense that they undermine or contradict orthodox Christian teaching. Is there anything else these ideas have in common? Are there, as Paul would argue, conscious strategies (the product of thinking, demonic minds) that lie behind them? I would argue that the ideas discussed above have several core beliefs in common – even when they appear to contradict each other.

1. Most of these ideas place man rather than God at the centre of his own universe. Each individual is therefore master or mistress of his or her destiny. God, according to these ideas, either does not exist or He should be ignored.

2. There is no need for salvation through Christ, these philosophies would say. This is because they would argue that "sin" does not exist. This is partly because many would argue that God does not exist, and therefore cannot judge sin; or that "sin" is really just human frailty caused by upbringing, genes, personality or circumstances. Human transformation, these philosophies

argue, is an improvement on what is already there, and accepted, in the individual's character: it is not achieved by the "putting to death" of man's "fallen nature" and the embracing of "newness of life" in Christ. If there is no need for salvation, then where is the need for a Saviour? These philosophies will all present Jesus as a "good man", perhaps even a "prophet" but never as the Incarnate God, who died to atone for a fallen creation.

3. According to these philosophies the Bible is neither inspired nor infallible. Therefore, what it has to say about why we exist, how we might change, and for what we are responsible is seen as debatable, outdated, or even simply wrong.

4. These philosophies regard Christian thinking, based on a revelation of God and of His Word, as simplistic, irrelevant or even deluded. That which is "modern" is viewed as innately superior – even when it is a re-hash of an ancient idea. This places pressure on the church to conform to current secular values: rather than let the Bible change us, the temptation is for us to change the Bible! The chief pressure on Christianity to conform to worldly ideas is in the area of personal morality.

5. Apparent contradictions between these philosophies (for example the "choice" of consumerism versus the "fatalism" of genetic determinism) simply disguise their common tendency to subordinate man from being a significant creature, made in the image of God, to the level of mere consumer or intelligent animal.

6. In none of these philosophies is there any other than arbitrary outcomes for human actions. There is no acceptance of the biblical concepts of heaven, hell, eternal consequences, biblical spirituality and righteousness, divine judgement, atonement, personal or national repentance. Man is free to act as he wishes, with only a legal system to keep him in check.

7. In the most modern of these philosophies, human beings are portrayed as existing in an ultimately meaningless universe. "Meta-narratives" (explanations that offer meaning to human existence, like Christianity) are written off as mere delusions.

8. Individual Christians, and sometimes entire Christian movements or denominations, can be strongly influenced, perhaps even "captivated" by one or more of these ideas.

9. None of these pathways leads to individual transformation or change, on God's terms. They either claim that change is unnecessary or that it can be achieved by the individual's will, to further his own needs or desires.

10. Moral values, according to many of these philosophies, are considered to be personal to the individual rather than being the absolute commands and paradigms of a holy God. This is why moral "goalposts" are frequently regarded as being legitimately "movable" in modern, Western society.

Overcoming "Big, Dangerous Ideas"

Practically, what can Christians do in the face of an onslaught of powerful, popular ideas? In 2 Corinthians 10:3-6 (GNB), Paul states that we have *"God's powerful weapons"* with which to fight these battles. What are these weapons?

The first, and greatest spiritual weapon in our armoury is our new, intimate relationship with the one true, Omnipotent God, our Heavenly Father, through and because of Jesus Christ. God is above all things and all things are under His ultimate control, no-matter how powerful they may seem to the world around us.

The second, wonderful, spiritual weapon we possess is the standing that we now have in Christ as believers - because of His atoning sacrifice for us:

"No, in all these things we have complete victory through Him who loved us!" [35]

Our personal and corporate victories are grounded in the spiritual consequences of Christ's suffering for us on the cross.

The third great spiritual weapon we have been given is the indwelling and baptising Holy Spirit, the third member of the Trinity. He grants power and spiritual insight to the believer:

"But when the Holy Spirit comes upon you, you will receive power…" [36]

Another great spiritual weapon is the inspired, infallible Word of God, the Bible. In Ephesians 6:17 the Bible is described as *"the sword the Spirit gives you"*. It is worth noting the other spiritual armour listed in Ephesians 6 – notably, in the context of taking false arguments captive, we have the "helmet" (protecting the mind) of "salvation".

In addition, we have the spiritual weapon of prayer, which is the outworking of those "weapons" listed above. The battle for a nation, a congregation, a family or an individual can only be "fought" through intercession. The genuineness of the concern we have for any person, place or issue is directly proportional to the amount of prayer (individual and corporate) that we offer up to God on behalf of people or issues that cannot or will not pray for themselves. The Bible is clear, God responds to "groaning" (genuine intercession), not to "moaning" (pontificating that gets us nowhere). A harbinger of great Revivals of Christianity in the past, was a marked increase in passionate intercession. May we see this today in our nations!

Yet another great weapon is the bold and anointed preaching of the full Gospel of Christ, which is frequently described in the New Testament as having power. Any substitute "gospel", or watering down of this Gospel will render our message powerless – the Gospel of Christ is the message the Devil does not want to be preached!

Other weapons given by God to the believer are sound, biblical teaching (as well as preaching), scriptural pastoral care and personal sanctification (including the renewal of the mind). Praise and worship are also important features of our spiritual warfare. The gifts of the Holy Spirit also provide the believer with powerful weapons. The fruit of the Spirit portray the qualities and characteristics of God's Kingdom, providing a positive alternative to the ultimate ineffectiveness of the philosophies mentioned in this chapter.

God will never leave us unarmed to fight a spiritual battle but – because the battle is spiritual – it cannot be won by human talent, intelligence or effort. Nor will it be won by viewing other human beings as our enemies. We must recognise our true enemy! Many Christians fight with one another, or write off human beings who are in the grip of the many delusions abroad in the world today. But the Bible says[37], *"For we are not fighting against human beings…"*. During the Troubles in N. Ireland we, who prayed, had to recognise that Christ died to save all sinners – including terrorists. The kind of praying that God led many of us into was graciously and miraculously answered, and it also encouraged a climate of greater reconciliation. Prayer against flesh and blood is forbidden in the Bible. God was moved by love to send His Son to save the "world". We also must love those who live in it – even those who persecute us.

Ultimately, it is only a new move of the Holy Spirit in a nation, through the church, that overcomes the power of these big, dangerous ideas. As the Gospel is preached in the power of the Holy Spirit whole communities can be translated from darkness into light.

CHAPTER 6

THE PRICE OF DISCIPLESHIP - OUR PART IN OUR TRANSFORMATION

Change is never easy or painless, even with God's help. Triumphing over external and internal adversities requires honesty, determination and humility. Above all, it requires constant openness to the working of the Holy Spirit in our lives. The Bible teaches us that salvation is free but to be a disciple means taking up our own personal crosses[1] and following Christ, wherever He leads. In this chapter we will explore some of the responsibilities we must embrace if we are to reign in life by His grace. I want to make this plain – I will speak of responsibilities, not striving. Striving will never achieve transformation, it will only produce frustration. Any meaningful and lasting change in us is only because of the wonderful grace of God. This process requires our co-operation with Him at all times.

Sanctification

I knew, on the night I became a Christian, that I had become a new creation in Christ and that the old life I had led had gone forever.

However, I also discovered that new birth is the beginning, not the end of a process. God continues to change me to this day, refining what He began in me all those years ago. This process of change, from dominant negative passions to increasingly godly motives and behaviour is often referred to as sanctification.

It was immediately obvious to me, as a new Christian, that the Holy Spirit had much work to do in my heart, mind and character. I knew that I needed to be changed. I also discovered what I have subsequently experienced many times since, that God has a unique way of convincing us of His love for us, whilst at the same time challenging us over some specific issue that He wants to change, Remember, God is not inclined to condemn Christians. Through Christ, He has justified us! However, whilst there is clear biblical evidence of the confidence we should now have in our standing in Christ, the New Testament never encourages complacency and it issues real challenges and warnings to converts. On the basis of His grace alone, I was shown that I could only be transformed by allowing the Holy Spirit full access to my life, by obeying God and by co-operating with Him fully.

The premise of all of these aspects of transformation is that, based upon the promises and covenants of God, the Holy Spirit is constantly at work within the believer, to work out the purposes of God. The Holy Spirit oversees this process in each disciple, in terms of what happens, how it happens and when it happens. Although the Holy Spirit can work suddenly and dramatically in our lives, we frequently have to be thankful and patient for gradual change over a period of time. Transformation, if it is to last, takes time!

The word "sanctification" is most often associated with "holiness", otherwise defined as an increasingly godly character. It does mean this but it also means much more. The Hebrew word that is consistently translated "sanctified" is *qadash*[2], which means "to make clean, appoint, consecrate, dedicate, hallow, purify or describe as holy". The Greek word that is just as consistently translated "sanctified" is *hagiazo*[3] , which means "to make holy, purify, venerate, sanctify, worship as awesome, sacred" (from *hagios*, "saint"). God is constantly at work within the submissive Christian disciple to purify him or her - body, soul and spirit.

For the Christian sanctification is a process that begins when we are born again into the Kingdom of God, enabling us to be set aside for a life of holiness, worship and service. This process also involves a lifetime of purification, of inner transformation, wrought by the Holy Spirit. This is a process whereby we offer our bodies willingly, as living sacrifices, to the God who made us and bought us back into His family and kingdom for His own purposes. He did this by paying for us with the blood of His own Son on the cross. It is important to remember that, in the New Testament as well as the Old, salvation is never seen merely as a negative – as only an escape from God's righteous wrath and the punishment of hell. Salvation does, vitally, mean these things but it is essentially portrayed in the Bible as a positive transformation of the individual from being an object of wrath, enslaved to base passions, to become an object of mercy and, by His grace, an adopted son or daughter of God - created for eternal fellowship with Him. In today's society purity of heart and behaviour are not valued very highly. May we find in Him a new hunger for sanctification!

Disciplined Disciples

There are many promises in the New Testament about the Christian disciple reigning in Christ. God was willing to delegate much authority to Adam. In Christ, as His ambassadors and equipped by the Holy Spirit, the Christian disciple has even greater delegated authority. The disciple learns to reign over himself or herself; and the disciple learns to reign in the midst of circumstances and to know the authority he or she now has because of his or her position in Christ:

> *"and raised us up with Him, and made us sit with Him in the heavenly places in Christ Jesus"* [4].

In order to reign over temptation and the residual negatives of heart and mind, we must learn who we are in Christ and we must become disciplined disciples.

Discipline is generally understood to be a system of externally imposed sanctions and rewards designed to modify behaviour. Any rewards and sanctions system is based on a set of values that are important to those imposing the discipline. A good example is our traffic laws: if we break the speed limit we are fined; if we do not we have a clean record. Discipline changes human behaviour for the benefit of others, as well as for the individual. For example, without speed limits people would drive as fast as they wish and more people would die as a consequence.

The Bible has numerous examples of externally imposed divine discipline, which is always communicated as being ultimately firm but loving, protective and instructive. This is in contrast with the generally negative view of discipline held in secular, Western societies. Most cultures agree that the ideal form of discipline is an internally motivated, self-discipline that has become a part of the character of the individual. Godly self-control is ultimately impossible outside of regeneration, according to the New Testament. Furthermore, without self-government it is impossible to govern oneself, anyone or anything else. How are we to acquire this quality of character? In 2 Timothy 1:7 Paul reminds Timothy of the nature and qualities of the Spirit he has received, as a disciple of Christ:

> *"For the Spirit that God has given us does not make us timid; instead, His Spirit fills us with power, love and self-control."* [5]

The word translated "self-control" here is *sophronismos*, which means "moderation", "self-control" or "a sound mind". The message here is that, because of the gift of the Holy Spirit, our characteristics should reflect His. Furthermore, our human emotions and thoughts are now controllable – we are not governed by them, we govern them by the power of the Holy Spirit and the loving exhortation and chastisement of our Heavenly Father.

The process of discipleship and transformation necessitates divine discipline, which modifies our behaviour and ultimately changes our characters:

> *"When we are punished, it seems to us at the time something to make us sad, not glad. Later, however, those who have been disciplined by such punishment reap the peaceful reward of a righteous life."* [6]

This passage is also clear regarding the motivation behind the discipline imposed by a loving father. This discipline is intended to train his sons or daughters and build moral character into them. Irresponsible parents will simply indulge or ignore their children, thus "spoiling" or neglecting them. The disciple's new life in Christ never fails because of any inadequacy or insufficiency in God's ability or promises. It may fail, or at least be delayed, because of our own frailties. This is why we have to "endure" and be "steadfast". Every biblical promise has a condition attached to it; we must take care to understand and fulfil the relevant condition when we seek to appropriate the promise. In order to receive God's promises, He requires an attitude of obedience, faith, co-operation and trust from those who are in Christ.

We saw, in Chapter 4, that complete mental assent to His promises – based upon a conviction born out of revelation – forms the basis of this required attitude. But God desires more than robotic obedience; His command is that we love Him with all our hearts (for what we love we will follow after, *"as the deer pants for the water"*[7]). This love is beautifully described in the Song of Solomon, which expresses, in allegorical form, the love of the individual Christian (and the church) for Christ:

> *"I charge you, O daughters of Jerusalem, if you find my beloved, that you tell him that I am sick from love – simply sick to be with him."* [8]

This love is so important to God that He commands the Ephesian church (in Revelation 2:4-6) to return to their first love, with dire judgement promised if they do not.

We could look at many New Testament passages that speak of our new responsibilities in Christ but one will have to suffice, so let us examine what Hebrews Chapter 12 teaches about discipline, conditions and appropriate responses. One way of understanding the responsibilities placed upon the disciple of Christ, in this Chapter, is to consider the series of commands that it expresses[9].

The first of these commands is expressed in the first verse, which states that we are to "*lay aside every weight and the sin that clings so closely*". We are to get rid of the unrighteous books, music, ornaments, habits or anything else that act like weights, which would slow us down as we walk God's pathway of truth. We are also to be aware of, and avoid, the deceptive sins that lie in wait for us every day. By contrast, the next verse commands us to fill our lives with inspiration, worship and faith-building revelation, by "*looking to Jesus, the pioneer and perfecter of our faith*". In verse 3 we are to "*Consider him who endured...*" so that we are strengthened to continue in our faith, even through trials and difficulties. Verses 4-6 remind us that Jesus paid for our redemption by His blood, and that God's discipline is a sign of His love, not His rejection. In verses 7-11 we are to "*Endure trials for the sake of discipline...*". Having endured, through trials, the disciple is commanded (v. 12) to, "*lift your drooping hands and strengthen your weak knees*". Tellingly, in verse 13 the disciple is then told to "*make straight paths for your feet*". The period towards the end of a trial is when it is easiest to give up. It is also a time for prayerful reflection and added determination about the course our lives are to take. Then the focus swings outwards; in verse 14 we are required to: "*Pursue peace with everyone, and the holiness without which no one will see the Lord*".

We are to obtain the grace of God rather than become like Esau (who "*sold his birthright*"). We must learn that nothing is more valuable than our relationship with God. In verses 18-24 we are asked to reconsider to Whom we have come and what is the nature of our new relationship with Him. What a glorious revelation and inspiration these verses offer!

Verse 25 sums up the desired response of the true disciple of Christ, *"See that you do not refuse the one who is speaking…"* The rest of the chapter reminds us that God is righteous and terrible in judgement as well as being gracious, loving and merciful.

The key message of this chapter is that because of who God is, and because of the sacrifice of His Son, our individual responsibility is to obey, co-operate with and trust in Him. In today's society everyone is looking for someone else to blame for their failures and misfortunes. You cannot blame anyone else if you fall short:

> *"His divine power has given us everything needed for life and godliness, through the knowledge of Him who called us by His own glory and goodness."* [10]

Tests and Trials

One of God's most effective means of building His character into us is through tests and trials:

> *"My brothers and sisters, consider yourselves fortunate when all kinds of trials come your way, for you know that when your faith succeeds in facing such trials, the result is the ability to endure. Make sure your endurance carries you all the way without failing, so that you may be perfect and complete, lacking nothing"* [11]

As a brand new convert I remember reading this passage for the first time, with bemused shock. I could not understand it at first as I thought that – having come to Christ – all my troubles were over! I simply could not understand how or why God would use painful trials of all kinds to transform the Christian disciple.

Through tests and trials, and the proper Christian responses during them, the righteousness of our characters is constantly being enhanced, whilst what is dross, in God's eyes, is being skimmed off.

To be skimmed off it has to come to the surface so that we can see the dross and renounce it.

"Tests" are testing situations, which demonstrate to us what we are really like – as opposed to how we would like to think we are! "Trials" are those fiery, difficult situations that – provided we respond to God correctly in them – will permanently transform our characters and personalities. In trials the grace of God is proven to have full effect in our lives. Some of the Hebrew or Greek words used in the Old and New Testaments can be translated as "test" *or* "trial" so the words can be very similar in meaning. When we read the Bible we see that all great men and women of God went through severe tests and trials.

Tests and trials always involve an examination of the value or truth of something by someone superior, who is equipped and authorised to do so. On occasion this evaluation involves an "assay" – that is, for example, a separation of the valuable ore from the dross by the application of chemicals or heat. During the Christian's testing process there is an analysis, as well as a judgement. There can be no doubt, also, that anyone undergoing such processes will be changed by the experience!

We must begin to understand tests and trials (none of which we like, or perhaps even want) by acknowledging that they are permitted by a sovereign and loving God. We have a tendency to think that everything that *feels good* is from God, whereas everything that *feels bad* is from the devil. This can sometimes be true – and we need to discern the difference between a spiritual attack and a godly trial - but it is categorically not true of tests and trials. Indeed, the first sign of God's approval of a sacrifice (even a living one, Romans 12:1) is to send heavenly fire down upon it to consume the flesh! When we fully surrender to God we are "baptised in (with) fire". This is a sign of divine acceptance, not rejection. The Bible also describes God as a "consuming fire". Furthermore, by being surrounded by divine fire – often experienced as fiery trials – the dross in our characters is consumed so that what is produced in us is pure gold. This is literally a refining process of the soul. Like Moses' burning bush we are not consumed by the trial. What is burned up is the flammable material of our worldliness!

Let us take, as an example, our natural lack of patience. The Bible says:

> *"We also boast of our troubles, because we know that trouble produces endurance, endurance brings God's approval, and His approval creates hope."* [12]

Another translation puts it this way, *"tribulation worketh patience…"*. If only you or I could take a tablet and suddenly be patient! That wish, in itself, indicates just how impatient we are! Rather, God puts us into situation after situation, where we are compelled to wait for something (or someone!). How we love to wait! This is real tribulation! (Though what is spoken of in Romans 5:3 is more serious than mere waiting.)

Have you ever noticed how much more compassionate you are, how much gentler, when you have gone through a serious trial, provided that you have resisted the temptations of bitterness, cynicism, self-pity or discouragement? Truly, as has often been said, tests and trials either make us better or bitter! A close study of the verses quoted above, from Romans, reveals the divine outcome of trials, if our attitudes during tests and trials are right.

It is also worth noting that Jesus invariably went through a test or a trial just before every major development in His ministry. For example, at the beginning of Matthew Chapter 4 Jesus was led *by the Spirit* into a wilderness, to be tempted by the devil. Having successfully overcome the devil in this trial, Jesus then began His public ministry, empowered by the Holy Spirit. Luke 4:14 describes Him thus, after His temptation:

> *" Then Jesus returned to Galilee, and the power of the Holy Spirit was with Him."* [13]

Unlike our trials, this test was not organised by His Father because Jesus needed to be purified. The trial was to demonstrate His obedience to His Father, and to teach us how to overcome the devil.

The result of this trial was great empowerment by the Holy Spirit, working through obedience. Jesus' trials also provide valuable lessons and encouragement to all of us. Consider, and be encouraged by, His response to these trials. What does Jesus' response teach us about the attitude God desires from us?

Firstly, we successfully come *through* the trial by immediately – and with sustained determination - putting our faith and trust completely in God. Sometimes we are forewarned about a trial (though more often, of an enemy attack). However, trials are frequently completely unexpected. In any case, the ferocity of the test or trial – the reality of its power to expose our vulnerability – is, at first, potentially overwhelming. Something we hear, or that happens to us, could destroy our faith or shatter our peace in a second, if we are not on our guard. As we enter the first moments of a trial we must give it over to God so that He might be glorified in it; and we must trust Him fully, to bring us out of it better and more blessed people than we went into it.

Secondly, we must begin to acknowledge the divine purpose of the trial and accept that God has allowed it to achieve the purpose, not of crushing us, but of improving us. As this process is worked out He will be with us for every step of the trial. Remember James 1:2-4 and Romans 5:3 – we are to rejoice in trouble! This does not just mean that we should praise Him *despite* the trouble, through gritted teeth; it means that we know that trouble is simply an opportunity to bring a fresh revelation of His grace. It also means that when we come to the end of our resources, that is when we begin to see miracles. I have learned so much more about God during times of trial than at any other time. The early Christian martyrs even equated trials with blessing and glory, though this is hard for the modern Western mind to comprehend!

Thirdly, we must co-operate with the Holy Spirit during the trial. We may need to repent, submitting to His guidance and healing power and to the fire that purifies. As well as the imputed righteousness of the Atonement, God wants to purify our hearts and minds. We will never become more like Christ than we are right now without absolute submission to our Father. If we are truly His, then He must be the potter and we must submit to become His clay, His workmanship.

Fourthly, remember God's character and promises throughout the trial. It is so easy, in the furnace, to grow disillusioned, angry and frustrated. All the while, our Good Shepherd is watching over us and He will lead us safely through frightening valleys full of shadows, to new spiritual pastures and waters.

Fifthly, remember that the devil will pay us particular attention in the trial. The Bible portrays him as being like a roaring lion, seeking someone to devour. We must not allow our spiritual guards to slip in the trial. The devil's purpose in the trial is to persuade us to deny God and so suffer pointlessly.

Sixthly, we should praise God continually and keep praying and reading our Bibles as much as we can. God is still there, even if we cannot *feel* His presence. He is just as real, just as constant, as He was at the moment of our greatest blessings.

Seventh, as we come out of the trial we should thank God for it and be determined not to forget the lessons we have learned in it. We must absorb these lessons, to help form a new righteousness in our minds and hearts.

At the end of September, 2004 I developed an undiagnosed but very debilitating illness. My doctor eventually concluded that I had Chronic Fatigue Syndrome. Although serious, as illnesses go it was not painful (nor immediately life-threatening). Its chief symptom was complete exhaustion. Prior to this illness I was very busy but very blessed. I do not remember feeling particularly stressed. Indeed, I had just come through a period of great blessing across a range of areas in my life. I had been blessed with good health all of my life. So this came out of the blue and it came at a very inconvenient time!

At first I could do very little as I was unconscious most of the time. But, little by little, I regained enough consciousness to seek God's face in the trial. He told me He would heal me, gradually (meanwhile Caroline, my dear wife, had independently received the same promise). He taught me how to hold on to His word, and use it to "slay" my "Goliath". He taught me how to rise up in faith at key times so that I was not submitting to the devil's plan for my life (which was to "*kill, steal and destroy*"). God also taught me much more, about divine grace and my absolute dependence upon Him. He taught me that it was more important to know Him than to serve Him; that in knowing Him I would serve Him with greater fruitfulness. And much more!

What a blessed time this was! Now, it was no joking matter: I suffered great physical, emotional and mental weakness. This was a very genuine, long and profound trial. It took years to recover from the illness and its effects. But my testimony is that I am a much richer person spiritually because of the trial (I leave it to others to evaluate whether I am a better person after it!). I am living proof of what I encourage above and I have found my God to be utterly faithful and trustworthy in transforming me. I have also learned that in times of great distress His Spirit is a true Comforter.

The Cross and Wholeness in Christ

We saw at the beginning of this book, from a brief consideration of Adam's creation in the first chapter of Genesis, that God made man a tripartite being: body, soul and spirit. We also saw that these three aspects of human identity are strongly interrelated. Adam's fall from grace, as a consequence of his sin, affected his body, his soul and his spirit. The redemptive work of Christ on the cross is complete, effective and final.

The chief outcome of this sacrifice on the cross was the testament, and the beginning, of a New Covenant between God and man, purchased by Christ's death and resurrection. Christ had to die on the cross as a perfect substitute, to pay the penalty for our sins. In this sense it was a merciful judicial act, fulfilling the just requirements of the Law to satisfy a Holy God, who could never condone or ignore unrighteousness. Jesus, the holy, spotless Lamb was sacrificed so that our sins could be forgiven. As we put our faith in Christ's atoning, cleansing, forgiving, reconciling sacrifice on the cross we are saved from the penalty of sin. Also, our relationship with God is – through grace – then placed on the footing of an adopted son or daughter (rather than suppliant sinner).

If that were the sum total of what was accomplished on the cross then it would still be extraordinarily gracious and astonishing. However, as I have said, the shedding of Christ's blood also sealed the beginning of a New Covenant, a "new" set of promises and conditions, made for man by God. Included in these promises is the new relationship men and women can have with their Heavenly Father, through the salvation we obtain in Christ. The benefits of this new relationship include on-going healing, revelation, liberation and sanctification. The price we pay is complete death to self.

To help us to understand this, let us look briefly at a few words that are translated "salvation" or "saved" in the Bible. In the Old Testament the most commonly used Hebrew word is phonetically represented as *yeshooaw*. This word is used, for example, in Genesis 49:18 and Isaiah 52:10. It has a broad range of meanings, including "deliverance", "aid", "victory", "health", and "welfare". In different contexts it can mean slightly different things but what is clear is that it means more than the forgiveness of sins.

The New Testament also makes many promises regarding wholeness, as well as forgiveness, for those who put their faith in the atonement of Christ and who experience, as a result, the new birth. This fuller sense of what was accomplished for mankind on the cross is also found in the two Greek words most commonly translated "salvation/saved". These words are *soteria* and *sozo*: the former word conveys the principal meanings of "deliver", "health" and "save"; the latter word can mean "rescue", "redeem" and "make whole". There is no disagreement amongst orthodox Christians about the comprehensive effectiveness of Christ's atonement, paid for by His crucifixion. Some Christians believe that "wholeness" will only be accomplished after death, when we enter fully into the resurrection of Christ. I believe, however, that the Christian begins to be made whole from the point of new birth onwards, and that this transformation is an on-going process. Note the implications, for example, of the promises communicated in Romans 8:11:

> "And if the Spirit of Him Who raised up Jesus
> from the dead dwells in you, [then] He Who raised
> up Christ Jesus from the dead will also restore to

life your mortal (short-lived, perishable) bodies through His Spirit Who dwells in you." [14]

Christ's resurrection provided proof of His atoning work on the cross. As a result of the new birth the Spirit - who raised Christ from the dead - now dwells in the believer. A result of this is that for believers our mortal (not resurrection) bodies have "life" restored to them but these bodies will be relatively short-lived. We await the gift of our resurrection bodies as a completion of God's promises.

The results of man's fall, in Adam, are fully cancelled by Christ's redemption. What is clear, then, is that salvation includes three main benefits for the believer in Christ. The first is forgiveness of sin – with the promise of eternal life, wholeness in Christ, and the continuing indwelling presence of the Holy Spirit. The second of these three benefits, wholeness in Christ, is made possible because of the first benefit. The third benefit is an intimate relationship with God our Father, through Christ and by the Spirit. It is clear from this – and many other New Testament passages - that the sacrifice of Christ, attested to by God through Christ's resurrection, immediately introduced the New Covenant, with all of its benefits. The Good News is not just judicially important, it also offers the hope of transformation and wholeness for the believer, from the new birth onwards.

One of the most frequently quoted Old Testament passages, which describes with amazing prophetic accuracy Christ's suffering and death on the cross, is Isaiah 53. What does this passage have to say about the effects of the Messiah's sacrifice? Isaiah 53 is a wonderfully graphic and accurate description of the Messiah as "Suffering Servant". This is an insight into the ministry of the Messiah – written centuries beforehand – that only the Holy Spirit could have inspired. It describes the Divine Messiah condescending to take on human form, to suffer in the flesh and to atone for sin. I personally find this to be one of the most moving and powerful of all Scripture passages.

The chapter begins with reference to the reliability of this prophetic account and the disbelief of many who would reject the message of the Messiah. In verse 2 Isaiah then predicts that people would have problems believing that Jesus is the Messiah, given His apparently ordinary human birth and growth – which would be without any worldly signs of glory. Verse 3 predicts that His life and death would be characterised by rejection and mockery. In verse 4 we are then given an insight into what His suffering on the cross would accomplish:

> *"Surely He has borne our griefs – sickness, weakness and distress – and carried our sorrows and pain [of punishment]. Yet we ignorantly considered Him stricken, smitten and afflicted by God [as if with leprosy]."* [15]

As we focus on the effectiveness of Christ's work on the cross we see in this verse a full range of benefits made accessible to us by faith. Christ's death enabled God to forgive our sins because of His penal substitution but He also bore our "griefs", our sickness, weakness and distress. Jesus died to make us whole, providing a full remedy for the effects of the Fall.

The best commentary on the Old Testament is the New Testament. Note the context in which Matthew quotes this verse from Isaiah, in Matthew 8:17. In the previous verse Jesus is recorded as having cast out many demons and healing those who were sick. Then this verse from Isaiah is quoted as prophetic proof of healing as a sign or proof of His ministry. In fact, as we read Isaiah 53 in full and then consider Jesus' ministry and the ministry of the apostles and disciples, and the ministry of the Early Church, it is clear that the Primitive (earliest) Christians understood Christ's sacrifice as immediately ushering in the New Covenant, with all of its promises regarding the possibility for the wholeness of man. Christ's immediate followers believed that they were to continue Christ's ministry in full – not merely a portion of it.

I believe that there are aspects of Christ's suffering that represent various aspects of God's gift of wholeness and healing for those who believe. For example, the physical pain that Christ endured and the curse of the Fall that He bore ushered in physical as well as spiritual healing. The rejection and isolation He suffered meant that He suffered, for us, all kinds of emotional wounds on the cross. And the crown of thorns – rammed on to His skull – reminds us of the promises made by God in both the Old and the New Testaments, regarding healing and redemption for the mind. This holistic interpretation of Christ's accomplishments on the cross makes sense of the connection between the atonement and the full range of promises expressed throughout the New Testament. All of these promises have as their source and their legitimacy the crucifixion of Christ. The controversial subject of physical healing has been dealt with extensively elsewhere but the subject of the healing and sanctification of the soul have received scant attention. That is why I took the time, in Chapters 3 and 4, to consider the healing and transformation of the heart and mind.

TRANSFORMED INTO THE LIKENESS OF CHRIST

God's Original Purpose for Man

By now we have established that God has a plan for our lives. He is transforming us *into* something better as well as *from* something worse. I believe that any close reading of the Bible will answer the questions posed in our Introduction. God is not merely transforming us to make us *feel* better, to make us more *popular*, or *wealthy*, to give us a better *career* or to make us *stars* in His Kingdom. No, He has a much higher, eternal purpose for our souls and spirits than any of these questionable ambitions! His objective is to transform us into the likeness of His Son, Jesus Christ. This means that the fullest understanding of salvation and redemption is to see these wonderful transformative acts of grace as being processes, not mere events. A process has a beginning but it also has an ultimate goal, which involves the glory of God.

What was God's original purpose for creating Adam? In Genesis 1:26(a) we are told:

"God said, 'Let Us [Father, Son, and Holy Spirit] make mankind in Our image, after Our likeness'…" [1]

When God created man, He created him uniquely, amongst all created things, to resemble Himself. The word "image" (*tseh-lem*) means "to resemble". The word is used of Seth, made in his father's image, in Genesis 5:3. The word "likeness" (*demuth)* implied for the Early Church Fathers a deeper sense of similarity, of nature and character. Let us pause and reflect for a moment, to consider what God's desire for man is, as expressed in His stated motivation in Genesis 1:26. God is Spirit, so we must not understand *likeness* in physical terms. Neither did God mean that He wanted to make mankind to be gods, although He gave Adam delegated authority over creation. What is clearly meant is that man was to be "like" God in character; inspired and enabled through a spiritual intimacy with his Maker. The value placed on man by God is seen, for example, in His view of the seriousness of murder:

"Whoso sheds man's blood, by man shall his blood be shed; for in the image of God He made man." [2]

Murder is especially heinous, not just because it robs another human being of his or her life but because man is made in God's image - so the crime of murder is a crime against God Himself.

The question must be asked, was the purpose of God, in creating Adam in His own image and likeness, intended for Adam only? Or perhaps God's ambition for man was deflected or altered by the Fall? God forbid! I believe that God's purposes are eternal and certain in intent and design and that His will remains steadfastly fixed on these purposes. God's desire, then, is still to make man in His own image and likeness. An interesting aid to understanding this is expressed in Hebrews 10:1, where the writer, inspired by the Holy Spirit, says:

"The Jewish Law is not a full and faithful model

of the real things; it is only a faint outline of the good things to come..." [3]

It is consistently stated in the New Testament that the Law served as a shadow of, and preparation for, the spiritual benefits of the New Testament, established in Christ. This New Covenant was made by a merciful God to redeem mankind to Himself and thus complete His original plan.

The first man, Adam, was made in God's image but fell. The second man, Christ, in His incarnation was fully human but did not sin. He thereby fulfilled the just requirements of the Law and, consequently, made a way for man to return to God to be transformed into God's image and likeness in his spirit and character:

> *"Thus it is written, The first man Adam became a living being – an individual personality; the last Adam (Christ) became a life-giving Spirit – restoring the dead to life. But [it is] not the spiritual life which came first, but the physical then the spiritual. The first man [was] from out of the earth, made of dust - earth-minded; the second Man [is] the Lord from out of heaven."* [4]

The Mosaic Law focuses on the externals of human behaviour, whereas regeneration in Christ makes possible an inner transformation of spirit and soul. This inner transformation is a radical change of spirit, heart and mind and, consequently, of behaviour.

God's Will Is to Transform You

I have often been encouraged by the promises of God in Isaiah 61:3, which I have already quoted in this book. In this verse God promises that, through the work of the Messiah, He will give to those who come to Him *"beauty for ashes"*, the *"oil of joy for mourning"* and *"the garment of praise for the spirit of heaviness"*, in order that they might become "*trees of righteousness, the planting of the Lord*". These promises tell us that we provide the "*ashes*" and God provides the "*beauty*" (a "bridal tiara"). Furthermore, the "*oil*" of healing joy is given to those who mourn; and a gracious ability to worship is given to the depressed or discouraged, enabling them to cast off a spirit of "*heaviness*"; and finally, our righteousness is explained as a gracious act of impartation and new birth *("planting")*. God is committed to transforming us, if we wish Him to!

There is a short New Testament passage, Ephesians 2:8-10, which beautifully explains the desire and provision of God for all who trust in Christ:

> *"For by grace are ye saved through faith; and that not of yourselves: it is the gift of God: not of works, lest any man should boast. For we are His workmanship, created in Christ Jesus unto good works, which God hath before ordained that we should walk in them."* [5]

The word "workmanship" is very illuminating. In Greek it is the word *poiema*, which is a word ("poem") that speaks of artistic creation, communication, function and beauty, all at the same time. From the moment we are born again into Christ we begin to become God's "poem", walking into and working out the good deeds He has prepared for us. Everything begins with Christ, and all will be accomplished through Him. But please remember, in Christ you are God's poem! The "re-drafting" of this poem will take at least a lifetime but the poem is already beautiful in God's sight because it expresses the wonderful grace and love of Christ, showing forth His handiwork. The child of God is a work of His art, telling forth the glory of the Divine Artist.

Transformed into The Likeness of Christ

Perhaps the earliest explicit expression of the Trinity, in the Bible, is contained in Genesis 1:26, which was quoted near the beginning of the chapter. In this text the creation of man is explained. *"Let us make man in our image"*, says Almighty God: one image, one substance, three persons in one. Man is made in the single image and likeness of our triune God. Man was always meant to be a visible expression of God's character, indicative of the Creator. When the second Person of the Trinity (Jesus) took on human form He looked like other men, and was fully human (as well as fully divine) except that He did not sin. This did not immediately make mankind more like God in character – individual, radical transformation is required for that to happen. But the possibility of it happening could only be achieved because Christ suffered an agonising death on the cross, to atone for our sins. Let us look at several biblical passages to understand this process.

In 2 Corinthians 4:4 Christ is referred to as the *"image of God"* (in Greek the word *eikon* is used for *"image"*). In Colossians 1:15 Christ is described in these terms again but then a link is made with mankind:

> *"He is the exact likeness of the unseen God – the visible representation of the invisible; He is the Firstborn – of all creation."* [6]

Christ, during the period of His incarnation, expressed the reality and nature of the unseen, spiritual God because Christ is God and because of His pre-eminence over all of creation. In His incarnation, Christ identified with the physical creation of space and time by taking on human form, by making God understandable to man, and by suffering on a cross to redeem that creation. Then, in Colossians 3:10, our insight is made complete:

> *"[You, who are in Christ] have clothed yourselves with the new [spiritual self], which is (ever in the process of being) renewed and remoulded into (fuller and more perfect knowledge upon) knowledge, after the image (the likeness) of Him who created it."* [7]

Thus those who put their trust in Christ will truly be transformed into the image and likeness of the invisible God. By changing us, God is not random in design, neither is He simply improving on what He finds in us. Rather, He is conforming us to a prototype – Christ Himself.

Another passage that wonderfully describes this process, and God's plan for our lives, is found in Romans 8:29:

> *"For those whom He [God] foreknew – of whom He was aware and loved beforehand – He also destined from the beginning (foreordained them) to be moulded into the image of His Son [and share inwardly His likeness], that He might become the first-born among many brothers."* [8]

Do not be distracted, for the moment, by questions about the meaning of "predestination"! What is clear from this verse is that God's purpose for those who are in Christ – who put their faith in His gracious atonement - is that they should become inwardly like Him and share the same Father, God. *"Many brothers"* also indicates that this extraordinary plan of transformation is for many, not simply for a tiny, spiritual elite. Indeed, this plan is for all of those who truly share, by faith, in Christ's salvation:

> *"And all of us, as with unveiled face, [because we] continued to behold [in the Word of God] as in a mirror the glory of the Lord, are constantly being transfigured into His very own image in ever increasing splendour and from one degree of glory to another; [for this comes] from the Lord [Who is] the Spirit."* [9]

If we pay careful attention to this wonderful Scripture, we see that those who are in Christ have no veil (a barrier that conceals) between them and God. As Christian disciples who dwell in God's presence and receive revelation of His glory, we are changed from the inside out into His likeness. So transformation comes from seeing God as He is, which inspires us to become like Him. This should give us all hope and joy, and move us to praise, worship and adoration. That a holy God has made such promises to such as us!

This all requires patience and hope, as well as faith, and a steadfast love for the gracious God who redeemed us from eternal destruction, to share in His everlasting glory. In order to receive this inheritance, we must allow Him to continue to transform us! This eternal perspective ought to give us hope as we grapple with those areas of our lives which we know God wishes to change.

Remember, He will do the changing, at His pace and in His way!

CHAPTER 8

GOD IS GLORIFIED BY YOUR TRANSFORMATION!

In Christ

It has always been God's desire to make, then mould, human beings for His eternal glory. In Isaiah 44:1-2 the prophet reminds us that God made and called Israel, out of the imperfect stock of Jacob, whom He then had to "mould". The words *asah* (make, produced, created) and then *yatsar* (mould or fashion – like a potter with clay) are used to describe this initial selective and creative act, followed by a process of transformation. The metaphor of the clay and the potter is used several times in the Bible to describe the relationship between God and His human creation. He has given us free wills, not to rebel against Him but to choose to accept His grace and discipline with joyful obedience. The clay has first to be *in* the potter's hands then it is *shaped* on the potter's wheel.

The key New Testament conditional phrase for this process is *in Christ*. This phrase refers to all those who have trusted in Christ as their Saviour and now form part of His body, the church. Christ is both the locus and the enabler, in and for, the work of transformation that we have been considering. The phrase "in Christ", or an equivalent phrase, occurs 227 times in the New Testament. This alone makes it a core theology for the Christian disciple. Moreover, when we consider the benefits that flow from being in Christ its importance is better understood. Let us consider just a few of these benefits.

The phrase "in Christ" is the condition that confers many promises to those who have this relationship with Jesus[1]. Note the intimacy and unity that the Bible expresses to describe this new relationship:

> *"We know that the Son of God has come and has given us understanding, so that we know the true God. We live in union with the true God – in union with His Son Jesus Christ. This is the true God, and this is eternal life."* [2]

We begin our transformation in Christ and will continue it in Christ, throughout eternity. In the first Chapter of Ephesians the significance of being in Christ is wonderfully portrayed on a heavenly, timeless canvas:

> *"Let us give thanks to the God and Father of our Lord Jesus Christ! For in our union with Christ he has blessed us by giving us every spiritual blessing in the heavenly world."* [3]

So, in Christ, we are now spiritually acceptable to God; we can commune with Him and have all the spiritual blessings and equipping that we need for this world and for eternity. In verse 10, he goes on to say:

> *"This plan, which God will complete when the time is right, is to bring all creation together, everything in heaven and on earth, with Christ as head."* [4]

This does not mean that all human beings will ultimately be saved . This error inspired an early heretical teaching, called *apokatastasis*. This teaching, that all created beings (including Satan) would eventually be saved, clearly contradicts the doctrine of eternal punishment and would seem to make grace null and void. What Ephesians 1:10 does mean is that those who are in Christ will be brought together under His headship into ever greater spiritual unity with one another and into increasing harmony with Him.

The only "place" of salvation, security, healing and holiness – for you and me – in space or in time is "in Christ".

For The Glory of God

The glory of God and its benefits for those who are in Christ are mentioned in numerous Scriptures, in both the Old and the New Testaments. God is eternally glorious, regardless of the age in which we happen to exist. That He should willingly share His glory in any measure with us is astonishingly gracious. Please tread humbly in this subject. Glory can only be given: it cannot be taken. What has the glory of God to do with our transformation, as disciples of Jesus Christ? Why does God want to transform us into the image of His Son?

Jesus took on humanity to himself so that through Him we might share in His divine nature and enjoy all the benefits of redeemed sons and daughters of God. But why did He do this? It was most definitely not because we deserved it – though we certainly needed it! One possible answer, based on an understanding of the love of God, can be explained by His intention to address grave, universal human need. He is a compassionate, merciful God who is transforming us into the image of Christ because in every way that is good and necessary for us. God is nullifying the negative effects of the Fall on His own creation by Christ's atonement:

> *"For the creation was subjected to futility, not of its*
> *own will but by the will of the one who subjected*
> *it, in the hope that creation itself will be set free*

from its bondage to decay and will obtain the
freedom of the glory of the children of God." [5]

We see in these verses from Romans a more profound reason for God's plan of salvation. Note the word "glory" in this reference. Glory is linked with "*freedom*" as part of the inheritance of "*the children of God*". The word "glory" is also an important element in the verse quoted at the beginning of this book (2 Corinthians 3:18). Our transformation is into an ever more glorious state because we are being changed into the image and likeness of our glorious Saviour. This verse is very instructive on how and into what we are being transformed. The verse states that in His presence we see God's glory "*as in a glass*". At this point it is interesting to link this verse with Hebrews 1:3: this idea is that we see "*in a mirror*" not ourselves but rather a reflected image of God. The verse in Hebrews states that Jesus "*reflects the glory of God and bears the very stamp of His nature*". As we behold Christ, the manifestation of God to man, we are transformed into His likeness. Let us lift up our eyes to see, by revelation, with unveiled faces, God made known to us in Christ. By steadily focusing on Him, not ourselves, the Holy Spirit changes us from one degree of glory to the next. According to Paul, in Ephesians 1:18, this is our inheritance in Christ.

In the meantime, as stated in the same chapter, we live for the praise of God's glory. Worship, in all of its forms, is our reason for living. Much of today's teaching, in the West, focuses on what we get out of salvation. The Bible clearly teaches these benefits but its ultimate message is that God is transforming us so that we can worship Him in the beauty of holiness; with all of our beings.

Another aspect of glory is referred to by Christ:

> "*The glory which thou hast given me I have given*
> *them, that they may be one as we are one, I in them*
> *and thou in me; that they may become perfectly*
> *one so that the world may know that thou hast*
> *sent me and hast loved them even as thou hast*
> *loved me.*" [6]

So the glory that is His is given to us so that we may become one, showing forth God's love, grace and glory to a needy world. Unity amongst believers is deepened by a revelation of the glory Christ has freely given to us[7]. The basis of God's dealings with man is grace, a grace that of itself reveals the glory of God and brings Him glory. This is seen in the Old Testament in His dealings with Israel:

> *"They are my own people, and I created them to bring me glory."* [8]

I believe that Israel, and also all of redeemed mankind, were created by God for His glory. This was and remains the ultimate purpose of all of creation. God could not be glorified in fallen man, so salvation is the means by which God can bring glory to Himself through redeemed man.

Glory is an attribute of God (Isaiah 28:5), therefore in all that He does, including creation, redemption and transformation, He is glorified. In a very wonderful way, God is fully glorified in all of His dealings with mankind. He is glorified as Creator; His attributes of compassion and love also bring Him glory (1 Samuel 2:8); and, ultimately, God is glorified in the atonement of His Son, who gave Himself in an extraordinary act of gracious love and mercy to redeem fallen man. God will be glorified even further by this act of atonement, when Israel responds more fully to the Messiah. Indeed, in Psalms 79:9 we see that salvation is not just for our sakes – it is primarily for the glory of God (again, in 2 Corinthians 4:15, God is glorified because of His abundant grace). In 2 Timothy 2:10 God promises salvation and glory for His elect. After salvation there is also glory (including increased praise) in knowing Him[9]. And God is glorified in bringing His children to full salvation[10]. God is glorified by our resurrection in Christ[11]. After the resurrection of the saints, God will be glorified when we will be presented to Him[12] and then again as He presents the church to Christ as His bride[13]. Then, God will be glorified as we dwell with Him throughout the ages, transformed into the likeness of Christ. The link between glory and transformation is beautifully summed up in the Scripture quoted previously:

> *"And all of us [Christians], with unveiled faces, seeing the glory of God as though reflected in a mirror, are being transformed into the same image from one degree of glory to another; for this comes from the Lord, the Spirit."* [14]

And we see, in Psalms 104:31, the pleasure God takes in all His works and the glory that is due to Him because of them:

> *"The glory of the Lord shall endure for ever: the Lord shall rejoice in His works."* [15]

"His works" include us! God created man in His own image and likeness; He did this to have fellowship with us. Eternal life is defined in John 17:3 not in terms of a place or an experience but rather of a relationship. To know God is to have eternal life. This "knowing" goes far beyond limited comprehension – it involves intimacy, revelation and worship. God does not *need* fellowship but He *desires* it, to express His grace and love towards man and to be glorified, in return, as He fully deserves. As God transforms us, we will find an ever-increasing unity and harmony with brothers and sisters in Christ, as well as with God the Father.

For His own glory, God refines the disciple of Christ so that greater intimacy between an imperfect man or woman and a holy God is made possible. This relationship is entirely based on God's grace and love, as we approach Him in the imputed righteousness we have in Christ. This ought to lead to our gratitude and adoration towards Him. From the very beginning, God created man and his environment to ensure that we should love God freely, out of choice. The marriage that will take place between Christ (the Groom) and the church (the Bride) will not be a forced or loveless marriage.

God has shed His love abroad in our hearts. From glory to glory, ever-increasing intimacy with God will be made possible as we submit to a process of constant transformation and refinement. The glorious relationship between God and His adopted sons and daughters will far exceed the quality of His former relationship with Adam and Eve. To God be the glory, throughout eternal ages!

> *"But God, who is rich in mercy, out of the great love with which He loved us even when we were dead through our trespasses, made us alive together with Christ – by grace you have been saved – and raised us up with Him in the heavenly places in Christ Jesus, so that in the ages to come He might show the immeasurable riches of His grace in kindness toward us in Christ Jesus."* [16]

God's plan for us is one of glorious transformation, into the likeness of His Son. He will accomplish this through well-established spiritual processes and crises, all of which are clearly taught in the Bible. I encourage you to co-operate with the Holy Spirit to follow ardently this pathway of abundant life towards an eternity spent in open revelation of Him. May the Lord bless you and keep you, and make His face to shine upon you, now and forever more, as you allow Him to transform you.

CHAPTER 9

CHANGED INTO HIS IMAGE (IN THE TWINKLING OF AN EYE)

Introduction

"In a moment, in the twinkling of an eye, at the last trump: for the trump shall sound, and the dead will be raised incorruptible, and we shall be changed." [1]

In Chapters 7 and 8 we explored two of the principal reasons why God is transforming us, and into what He plans to transform us. We learned that He will transform us into the likeness of Christ, for His glory. In this final chapter we will consider two more goals God has for our transformation. God's plan is for the church to grow further into its role as a royal priesthood; and God has also destined us to reign in Christ. In order to equip Christians for both these roles of service, God will completely change us at the moment we are resurrected or raptured to meet with Christ, face-to-face. This phenomenal experience will complete a process that began with new birth and will usher in our fellowship with God, in its fullest sense, for all eternity.

In this chapter we will be given privileged glimpses by the Bible into our future destiny in Christ. We will see, with joy, certain clear promises that are made to all those who trust in Him. However, a note of caution must be struck at this point. Even the Bible does not fully draw back the curtain on the future; so, many fine Christians have radically different interpretations of the same prophetic passages. As the Apostle John says:

> *"My dear friends, we are now God's children, but it is not yet clear what we shall become. But we know that when Christ appears, we shall be like Him, because we shall see Him as He really is."* [2]

A close study of this verse helps our understanding of this future event. These promises are for those who are *"now God's children"*; that is, those who have by faith entered into new birth in Christ, followed by further transformation, as discussed in earlier chapters. Then John humbly states: *"it is not yet clear what we shall become"*. There is a necessary limit to our current knowledge of what we shall become in Christ. This ought to reassure us if we are struggling with this mystery of transformation. The mystery will become abundantly clear as we remain in Christ, and we will understand this new state into which we will enter when it happens (we live by faith, not by complete understanding). Furthermore, we are promised that we shall be made *"like Him"* because *"we shall see Him as He really is"*. At this critical point of transformation we will actually meet the risen Christ. We will no longer rely on partial revelation, nor on necessarily incomplete knowledge but we will enter into a relationship with Him that is more real, palpable and intimate. This will be a relationship even better than God had with Adam in Eden (because we will also have the knowledge of grace). Throughout the New Testament, men and women were changed by meeting Christ, sometimes in unpredictable ways (such as the fisherman whose reaction to a miracle was to cry out, *"Go away from me, Lord! I am a sinful man,"* [3]). Meeting Christ not only reveals His nature – it also reveals ours!

So we will need radical transformation to make us fit to fellowship with Him more fully, as His royal priesthood and as His joint heirs. What will be the nature of this transformation and when will it happen?

A Spiritual Body

As a boy of about nine or ten I suddenly developed an interest in how plants germinate and grow. I asked my father if I could use a small section of his garden, to plant some seeds? He kindly agreed and I bought a packet of sunflower seeds. They did not look very promising. They were dark, wizened and apparently lifeless. Nevertheless, in faith, I sowed them as instructed and - to my eventual joy – amazingly tall, vibrant and dramatic plants grew and blossomed. I have ministered quite a bit in Provence, France, in recent years and in that region they grow sunflowers as a cash crop. Northern Ireland is not Provence! But even in our wet and cold climate there was some inherent, irresistible life force hidden in those seeds that – given soil, moisture and air – produced a plant unrecognisably superior to the seed from which it sprang. Paul uses precisely this comparison – of seed and plant – to illustrate the difference between the bodies we have now and the resurrection bodies we will be given at the end of this age.

> *"Listen to this secret truth: we shall not all die,*
> *but when the last trumpet sounds, we shall all be*
> *changed in an instant, as quickly as the blinking*
> *of an eye. For when the trumpet sounds, the dead*
> *will be raised, never to die again, and we shall all*
> *be changed.."* [4]

In 1 Corinthians 15:35-58 we are told about our new resurrection bodies. And we are told when we will receive them. Paul's extended metaphor of the seed and the plant conveys the amazing difference between our present, perishable bodies, and our new, resurrection bodies. Verses 35-41 speak of the dead in Christ awaiting His return, which will trigger this amazing transformation. When they are caught up to meet Him they will be changed in an instant. Verse 42 states that these new bodies will be *"imperishable"* and that they will be characterised by glory and power. In verse 44 the new, resurrection bodies we will receive are referred to as *"spiritual"* bodies – formed to live more fully in God's presence. These spiritual bodies - thank God – will be completely superior to our present, perishable bodies. Verses 45-50 explain this teaching with respect to Adam and Christ: because of Adam we inherited bodies formed from the dust; and because of Christ we will share fully in His resurrection so that we will then be truly like Him. Forget the myth of Christians being wafted up into the sky, to sit on soggy clouds, strumming harps. The truth is much more exciting than that! When we are changed into His likeness (verse 49) we will not only receive new, spiritual bodies; we will also be made more like Him morally and mentally. Further renewal of our souls will take place.

Verse 51 of 1 Corinthians 15 reveals a truth previously hidden from mankind: that this amazing transformation – from perishable to imperishable; from physical to spiritual - will occur when the "last trumpet" sounds. At that point the dead in Christ will meet with Him and be transformed in an instant. Verses 54-57 form a hymn of praise as death and sin will be finally conquered at this resurrection.

But what of those Christians who will be alive at that future date? Paul wrote to the Thessalonians about this group of expectant, living disciples:

> *"What we are teaching you now is the Lord's teaching: we who are alive on the day the Lord comes will not go ahead of those who have died. There will be the shout of command, the archangel's voice, the sound of God's trumpet and the Lord Himself will come down from heaven. Those who have died believing in Christ will rise to life first, then we who are living at that time will be gathered up along with them in the clouds*

*to meet the Lord in the air. And so we will always
be with the Lord."* [5]

This passage tells us clearly that those who are alive at the time of
Christ's coming in the clouds will be *"gathered up along with them* [those
dead in Christ – who await His return] *"*. Subsequent to this amazing
transformation *"we will always be with the Lord"*. This should inspire
all those who have believed in Him to rejoice for evermore. To worship
Christ with our new, resurrection bodies after the transformation
discussed above will transcend even the most wonderful time of praise,
worship and blessing we have ever experienced.

A Royal Priesthood

This idea of eternal worship and service brings us to our present
and future roles as a royal priesthood[6]. The title implies that we are to
worship and serve one who is both King and God. This, of course, is
Christ. Have you ever noticed that, during Christian services, the Holy
Spirit becomes very interested when we exalt Christ but tends to "leave
the room" when we exalt a man or a movement? The most holy creatures
of this present age understand this truth:

> *"Round Him [the Lord] flaming creatures were
> standing, each of which had six wings. Each
> creature covered its face with two wings, and its
> body with two, and used the other two for flying.
> They were calling out to each other
> 'Holy, holy, holy!
> The Lord God Almighty is holy!
> His glory fills the world'."* [7]

These amazing angelic creatures, each with six wings, stand in
the very presence of God. Their service is to worship God perpetually.
Notice their humility, as they cover themselves with four of their six
wings, out of adoration for the God in whose presence they stand.

We, as disciples of Christ, already serve and worship Him – out of a revelation of who He is. We have already seen that revelation brings insight and transformation; it also inspires worship. How much better will we be equipped to serve and worship Him because of our new resurrection bodies, and because we will be made like Him, morally and mentally, in the *"twinkling of an eye"*.

Joint Heirs with Christ

God always intended His redeemed saints to overcome, in Him, all the negative consequences of the Fall. Adam was called to serve God by caring for and ruling over God's creation[8]. Before he fell Adam lived in a state of innocence in intimacy with God and in physical, emotional and mental health. He exercised delegated authority and stewardship over all he surveyed. God's amazing promise for redeemed mankind is that we will not only reign *under* Him, we will also reign *with* Him. Just as man was originally given stewardship over God's creation, so redeemed man will also simultaneously serve and reign in Him:

> *"He who conquers, I will grant him to sit with me*
> *on my throne, as I myself conquered and sat down*
> *with my Father on His throne."* [9]

As the world awaited a Redeemer, Old Testament prophets were given privileged glimpses into the future restoration of man to his position of delegated authority:

> *"But the saints of the Most High shall receive the*
> *kingdom, and possess the kingdom for ever, for ever*
> *and ever…And the kingdom and the dominion*
> *and the greatness of the kingdoms under the*
> *whole heaven shall be given to the people of the*
> *saints of the Most High; their kingdom shall be an*
> *everlasting kingdom, and all the dominions shall*
> *serve and obey them."* [10]

And, as we have previously seen, those who have surrendered their lives fully to God will reign with Him, provided they endure:

"If we have died with Him, we shall also live with Him; if we endure, we shall also reign with Him; if we deny Him, He also will deny us." [11]

We are to believe that we can endure, by His grace because, *"whatever is born of God overcomes the world "*[12].

As we await the transformation that will take place at our resurrection or rapture, we need to celebrate the fact that – because of grace – we *"reign in life"*[13]. The New Testament declares that we are already *"more than conquerors"*[14] because, in this life, we have obtained by faith all of the relevant promises of God in Christ. His grace has already empowered us to enter into the position of adopted sons – as joint heirs with Christ[15]. Our transformation, at new birth and thereafter, makes us fit and equipped to reign. We needed to develop the character of kingdom rulers, not just to receive His authority. Authority without character is a dangerous thing. This godly character, with God's grace, allows us to overcome every trial we face.

In the Book of Revelation the constant condition and imperative, for gaining all the wonderful promises recorded there, is that we must be *"overcomers"*[16]. This word connects our present with our future, pointing as it does to the Christian's requirement to endure and gain victory over every spiritual enemy and every opposing circumstance. We overcome because of what Christ has done for us, because of our transformation in Him, and because of the constant and sufficient grace provided for us by God.

Then, at a future point in time, when we receive our resurrection bodies, we will gain a final victory over death and the "sting" of sin:

"O death, where is thy victory? O death, where is thy sting? The sting of death is sin, and the power of sin is the law." [17]

What of our lives after resurrection? This question takes us into consideration of a future period of time known to Christians as the millennium – the thousand year reign of Christ on this earth. There are three popular interpretations of what the Bible says about the millennium[18] . However, whichever interpretation you subscribe to, what is clear is that Christians are to play a distinctive role during this period. The most relevant portion of the New Testament is Revelation Chapter 20. During this thousand year period Satan will be bound (v. 2-3); nameless people will be empowered to judge (v.4); martyred saints will reign with Christ (v.4); those otherwise dead will be resurrected after the millennium (v.5) and they will then be judged according to great books of works and life (v.12).

Then, in Revelation 21, the Bible speaks of the redemption of heaven and earth as the old are replaced with the new. The new Jerusalem will descend from heaven and God will dwell with man. This will usher in a further deepening of intimacy between God and His people. Suffering, pain and death will be no more. There is also evidence in this chapter that the presence of sin will be removed, as those transformed in Christ will dwell forever in the light of His presence.

Throughout this entire process of transformation – from new birth to eternity – it is God's grace, not our goodness, that will change us from one degree of glory to the next. We need the help of the Holy Spirit to understand, even in part, what God has stored up for our eternal futures in Christ. Paul prayed for two necessary revelations for the Ephesian Christians. He wanted them to know the love of God (Ephesians 3:14-19) and he also prayed that they might glimpse their inheritance in Christ (Ephesians 1:15-23). I encourage you to pray these prayers for yourself, so that the revelation of who you are, or can be, in Christ might transform you.

Eternity Is Forever

It is very difficult for us to visualise or comprehend eternity. As we have seen, in Daniel 7:27, the kingdom of "*the people of the saints of the Most High*" will be an "*everlasting*" kingdom; but to help us to understand this concept of endless time, verse 18 expresses eternity this way, *"the saints of the Most High will receive the kingdom for ever, for ever and ever…"*. So time will become unimportant for us and our spatial environment will be utterly changed. Time and space aid man in his attempt to measure and understand his current existence. But in the final chapter of the Bible we are told of two very different experiences of eternity, one for those who are in Christ and one for those who have rejected Him:

> *"There shall no more be anything accursed, but the throne of God and of the Lamb shall be in it [the heavenly Jerusalem], and His servants will worship Him; they shall see His face, and His name shall be on their foreheads…Outside are the dogs…"* [19]

Kept for true disciples is an amazing destiny: we shall reign with Christ forever, serving Him and worshipping our Father God in His very presence. Forever we will be free from grief, bitterness, anger and fear because of the transformation of our minds and hearts. Forever we will know no pain, sickness or death because we will have spiritual, imperishable bodies. And forever we will be free from sin, its power and its presence, living in a state of perpetual and absolute grace.

All because of Christ's sacrifice for us, on the cross. Praise Him!

STUDY QUESTIONS FOR EACH CHAPTER

Chapter 1: Some Foundational Truths

1. How does the biblical account of the creation of man differ from other popular beliefs about the origins of humanity and what is its true significance?

2. Why did God create Adam and Eve?

3. Honestly consider the pathway your life is taking at the moment. Is it the way God would wish the rest of your life to take? What paths are your friends on?

4. How – in practical terms - do the Bible and the Counsellor (the Holy Spirit) help you to "walk" in the "way" that God wishes you to walk?

5. Prayerfully and privately consider which "bent" in your life could lead you off God's path, unless it is seriously addressed, with God's help?

6. In what areas does your knowledge and understanding of key foundational truths need to improve?

Chapter 2: The Necessity for Change and God's Gracious Provision

1. How does your understanding of the spiritual blindness of man help to inform your intercession? How does this spiritual blindness hinder evangelism?

2. Which part of the process of salvation is most neglected today? Why?

3. Discuss the meaning and importance of divine grace.

4. Is there a current need in your life for repentance? Given a fuller understanding of the word, what do you need to do about it?

5. How important is it to "feel different", after new birth?

6. What does this chapter tell you about the help available to you, from God, as you continue to be released from the power of sin?

Chapter 3: Binding Up The Broken Heart and Developing A Heart That Is Pleasing To God

1. What was your emotional state before becoming a Christian?

2. How did becoming a Christian affect you, emotionally?

3. Are feelings important to God?

4. What are the limitations of feelings?

5. What is the difference between the fruits of the Holy Spirit and their worldly equivalents?

6. How and for what purpose will God make your heart whole?

Chapter 4: The Christian Mind

1. Do you believe that your mind can be of any use to God? If so, how?

2. How do you strike the balance between using the renewed mind and sustaining dependence upon God for guidance in all things?

3. What do you most need revelation for at the moment? How will you obtain it?

4. What do the two prayers recorded in Ephesians teach us to pray for other Christians?

5. What part do Christ's atonement, the Bible and the Holy Spirit play in renewing your mind?

6. What mental battles are currently being fought in your mind? How does the Bible state that you will gain a victory?

Chapter 5: Pathways of Deception (Big, Dangerous Ideas)

1. Which of these "big, dangerous ideas" is/are most popular in the area in which you are living or ministering?

2. How can you use this information to make your evangelism more relevant?

3. Are you personally battling with any of these ideas at the moment?

4. What are the mighty spiritual weapons with which the Christian is supplied to "take every thought captive to Christ"?

5. Which of these deceptive ideas has most influenced Christian thinking, in your experience?

6. Which of these ideas will conflict most with Christianity over the next ten years (you may, of course, add to the ideas covered in this chapter)?

Chapter 6: The Price of Discipleship – Our Part In Our Transformation

1. Why is sanctification so rarely taught and how important is it?

2. What does it mean to be "made holy" in the Christian sense?

3. In what ways does God want us to be disciplined?

4. Is Christian discipline imposed by God or voluntarily accepted by us?

5. What should our attitude be when we are tested?

6. What does "wholeness in Christ" mean to you?

Chapter 7: Transformed into The Likeness of Christ

1. How does understanding God's original purpose for mankind influence your sense of identity and your sense of destiny?

2. How do you know it is God's will to transform you?

3. Discuss some other philosophies or religions that offer transformation? In what ways is Christianity superior to them?

4. If you had your choice, in what ways would you be transformed?

5. What is God's ambition/goal for your transformation?

6. Discuss how radical God's plan is for Christians and how it will be achieved?

Chapter 8: God Is Glorified By Your Transformation

1. What do you understand is meant by the phrase "in Christ"?

2. What does the Bible teach about those who are not "in Christ" and what should our response be to this?

3. How does your understanding of this term ("in Christ") inform your understanding of what happens to the Christian after physical death?

4. What is meant by the term "the glory of God"?

5. How can any man bring glory to God?

6. Why is it crucial to understand that your transformation is not only, nor is it primarily, for your own benefit?

Chapter 9: Changed Into His Image (In the Twinkling of An Eye)

1. What does physical death mean for the Christian?

2. Having taken a lifetime to be changed how will we be changed "in the twinkling of an eye"?

3. Why do our characters need to be changed to wield divine authority?

4. What will it mean to be part of a royal priesthood for ever?

5. Do you believe that the process of transformation will end when we meet Christ?

6. What does the Bible teach us about eternity?

REFERENCES AND NOTES

(Bible references are in **bold** when they have been quoted, in whole or in part)

Introduction: Is Change Necessary and Possible?

1. John 8:32
2. **Isaiah 61:3 (KJV)**
3. **Ephesians 2:10 (KJV)**

Chapter 1: Some Foundational Truths

1. **Hebrews 11:3 (GNB)**
2. Psalms 103:1-2
3. John 4:24
4. **Genesis 2:7 (GNB)**
5. The Hebrew word *neshamah,* translated here as "breath", can also mean "spirit" and is translated into English as "spirit" in Proverbs 20:27; the other common word for "breath/spirit" is *rewach* e.g. Job 27:3.

6. Genesis 1:26-30 There is nothing anti-environmental about God's intentions for man's stewardship of nature; man was intended to care for, not corrupt and exploit, the rest of creation.
7. **1 Thessalonians 5:23 (GNB)**
8. **Genesis 3:3-4 (GNB)**
9. **Genesis 3:7-8 (AB)**
10. **Ephesians 2:4-7 (GNB)**
11. **Psalms 101:2 (KJV)**
12. **Psalms 119:105 (KJV)**
13. **Psalms 119:35 (KJV)**
14. **Hosea 2:6 (KJV)**
15. **Isaiah 59:7 (KJV)**
16. Proverbs 20:24
17. Acts 2:28
18. Luke 1:79
19. Romans 14:17;
20. **Hebrews 12:13 (KJV)**
21. **Job 23:10 (KJV)**
22. Job 42:5-6
23. **Romans 8:1 (KJV)**
24. **Romans 8:8 (KJV)**
25. John 8:12 (KJV) *"...I [Jesus] am the light of the world: he that followeth me shall not walk in darkness, but have the light of life."*
26. **Hebrews 11:6 (GNB)**
27. **Proverbs 3:5-6 (KJV)**

Chapter 2: The Necessity for Change and God's Gracious Provision

1. **Psalms 14:1-3 (GNB)**
2. **2 Corinthians 4:4 (GNB)**
3. **Psalms 73:2 (GNB)**

4. Matthew 5:45
5. **Psalms 73:16-17 (GNB)**
6. **Jeremiah 17:9-10 (GNB)**
7. **Romans 2:4 (KJV)**
8. **John 1:17 (AB)**
9. **Ephesians 1:8 (AB)**
10. **Romans 3:24 (AB)**
11. **Romans 8:32 (AB)**
12. Ephesians 2:9
13. **Hosea 1:2 (NRSV)**
14. **Hosea 11:8 (NRSV)**
15. **Romans 2:4 (KJV)**
16. **Jude 15 (KJV)**
17. **John 16:8 (KJV)**
18. **Ephesians 5:13 (AB)**
19. **Psalms 88:7 (KJV)**
20. **Luke 5:8 (GNB)**
21. **Luke 13:3 (AB)**
22. **Luke 3:8 (KJV)**
23. **Job 19:25 (AB)**
24. **Romans 8:3 (AB)**
25. **2 Corinthians 8:9 (AB)**
26. **Romans 8:15 (KJV)**
27. **John 1:12-13 (KJV)**
28. 2 Corinthians 5:17
29. **2 Peter 1:4 (KJV)**
30. **John 3:3 (AB)**
31. **John 3:5-6 (AB)**
32. **Romans 6:3-4 (KJV)**
33. **Romans 7:6 (KJV)**
34. **Romans 8:13 (KJV)**
35. **1 John 1:7 (KJV)**
36. **Revelation 22:11 (KJV)**
37. **Revelation 7:14-17 (KJV)**

Chapter 3: Binding Up The Broken Heart and Developing A Heart That Is Pleasing to God

1. Galatians 4:19
2. **Psalms 35:13 (GNB)**
3. **Mark 12:33 (GNB)**
4. Psalms 42:1
5. Psalms 49:8
6. **3 John 2 (NRSV)**
7. **Isaiah 61:1-2 (GNB)**
8. **Romans 6:16-18 (KJV)**
9. **Ephesians 2:3 (KJV)**
10. **Galatians 5:22-23 (KJV)**
11. **Ephesians 3:16-19 (KJV)**
12. **Romans 14:17 (GNB)**

Chapter 4: The Christian Mind

1. Matthew 4:1-11
2. "discerning of spirits" is one of the nine gifts of the Spirit listed in 1 Corinthians 12:8-10; this gift is essential if we, as Christian disciples, are to "test the spirits" (1 John 4:1) and if we are to have an accurate awareness of the spiritual reality that exists around us.
3. **Philippians 4:6 ((GNB)**
4. **Hebrews 1:1-2 (GNB)**
5. The first word to consider is *nous*, which refers to the seat of reflective consciousness, including our faculties of perception, understanding, feeling, judging and determining (Romans 7:23 and 25). A second word is *dianoia,* the process of thinking something through, or meditation, for example Hebrews 8:10, 1 John 5:20 (cf. *sunesis*: ideas coming together to create understanding, Ephesians 3:4). Thirdly, *ennoia* refers to an idea, notion or intent (1 Peter 4:1). Fourthly, *noema* is a design or a constructed thought (Philippians 4:7). Fifthly, *gnome* refers

to a purpose, judgement or opinion (Philemon 4). Sixthly, *phronema* speaks of the content or focus of the mind (Romans 8:6). Finally, *phronesis* speaks of understanding that leads to right action (often translated "wisdom" or, as in Ephesians 1:8 "prudence").

6. **Romans 7:25 (KJV)**
7. **2 Corinthians 1:17 (KJV)**
8. To paraphrase some of the biblical promises regarding the mind, with Scripture references: the human will is to become subordinate to the Lordship of Christ (James 4:7); the reflective faculty can be enriched by meditating on Christ and His word (Colossians 2:2); the imagination can be used by God for revelation and the communication of Spiritual Gifts (Acts 2:17-18); the interface between the mind and the emotions can become an avenue for healing (Isaiah 26:3); the contents of our minds constantly need adjusting (Philippians 4:8); the mental habits, or "grooves", of the mind can be taken captive and transformed in Christ (2 Corinthians 10:5); our consciences, our "inner courtrooms", need to accept Christ as our mediator (Romans 8:31-34); our memories need to be cleared of guilt, with all wounds dealt with by the blood of Christ (Romans 8:1), and we need to remember the goodness of God (Psalms 103); human creativity, when directed by the Holy Spirit, can be inspired to produce praise and worship of all kinds, and can be used by God for evangelism (Psalms 146:1), the interfaces between our minds and passions need to experience godly discipline, sanctification, forgiveness and renewal (Ephesians 4:22-24). This list is comprehensive but not exhaustive. I would encourage you to make your own study of this subject, using the Bible as your source book.
9. **Romans 7:23 (KJV)**
10. **Galatians 3:23 (KJV)**
11. **Hebrews 8:10 (KJV)**
12. **1 Corinthians 1:18 (AB)**
13. **2 Corinthians 4:16 (AB)**

14. **Ephesians 4:23 (AB)**
15. **Romans 8:6 (KJV)**
16. **1 Peter 4:1 (KJV)**
17. **1 Peter 1:13 (KJV)**
18. These benefits include: unity of purpose, thought and focus (Romans 15:6, 1 Peter 3:8); our memories are sanctified (Philemon 4, Mark 14:72); our hopes and opinions are inspired by God's compassion for others (Acts 15:37); we will make sense to other believers if not always to the world (2 Corinthians 5:13).
19. **Philippians 4:7 (KJV)**
20. 1 Timothy 4:6
21. Hebrews 8:10; Hebrews 10:16
22. **Philippians 4:8 (GNB)**
23. **Colossians 1:13-14 (GNB)**
24. **1 John 5:20 (KJV)** (cf. 2 Corinthians 4:4)
25. **Luke 24:45 (KJV)** (cf. Ephesians 1:18-19)
26. **Ephesians 6:13 (KJV)**
27. **Colossians 3:2 (GNB)**
28. **Revelation 12:11 (RSV)**

Chapter 5: Pathways of Deception

1. **Matthew 7:13 (GNB)**
2. **2 Timothy 3:1 (GNB)**
3. Matthew 8:28
4. **Proverbs 14:12 (GNB)**
5. **2 Corinthians 10:4-5 (GNB)**
6. **2 Corinthians 11:14 (AB)**
7. **John 14:6 (GNB)**
8. **Luke 12:19 (GNB)**
9. **Ecclesiastes 6:2 (KJV)**
10. **Luke 12:19-20 (GNB)**
11. **Luke 12:15 (GNB)**
12. **1 John 3:17 (GNB)**
13. **Romans 12:1 (GNB)**

14. **1 Chronicles 16:29; Psalms 29:2; Psalms 96:9 (RSV)**
15. 1 Corinthians 12:13
16. Revelation 22:17
17. **Romans 6:15 (GNB)**
18. **Hebrews 11:1 (GNB)**
19. **Job 15:1-3 (GNB)**
20. **Nehemiah 4:1-3 (GNB)**
21. **Ephesians 2:3 (AB)**
22. **Romans 6:16 (GNB)**
23. **Deuteronomy 18:10-12 (GNB)**
24. **Revelation 22:18-19 (GNB)**
25. Matthew 7:15
26. **2 Peter 2:1 (GNB)**
27. **Matthew 24:24 (GNB)**
28. Those interested in exploring this subject further might wish to study the Book of Revelation, Matthew 24, 1 Thessalonians 4, and 2 Thessalonians 1-2, (as well as the Old Testament Prophets).
29. Matthew 4:1-11
30. 2 Thessalonians 2:3
31. **Romans 13:10 (KJV)**
32. **Matthew 5:21-22 (KJV)**
33. Luke 6:28; 1 Corinthians 4:12
34. **Matthew 6:10 (KJV)**
35. **Romans 8:37 (GNB)**
36. **Acts 1:8 (GNB)**
37. **Ephesians 6:12 (GNB)**

Chapter 6: The Price of Discipleship – Our Part in Our Transformation

1. Luke 14:26-27
2. The full significance of the Hebrew word is borne out by its use in the Old Testament. In Genesis 2:3 the seventh day was

sanctified by God (set apart for His use). In Exodus 19:14 people are cleansed and forgiven (purified), and in Exodus 29:43 God's presence sanctifies (all sanctification comes from Him). In Leviticus 8:15 oil (a type of the Holy Spirit) is used to sanctify (cf. Numbers 7:1 and 2 Chronicles 29:19). In Leviticus 10:3, Numbers 20:13 and Isaiah 5:16 God is sanctified by those who come to Him (He is worshipped, hallowed, venerated by them). God sets aside (sanctifies) certain men as His own, in Numbers 8:17 and 1 Samuel 7:1, 16:5. In 1 Chronicles 15:14 the priests sanctified themselves for a particularly holy task and in 2 Chronicles 7:16 and 29:17 God sanctifies His house. In Ezekiel 20:41 the nation of Israel is sanctified, or set apart for God's special purposes.

3. For those under the New Covenant this term is just as important. The key to understanding its New Testament significance is to appreciate that we are sanctified fundamentally by the atoning blood of Christ. A few verses will suffice to show us other aspects or expressions of this sanctification: we are sanctified by the Word of God (1 Timothy 4:5); we consciously submit to this spiritual process (2 Timothy 2:21); we are purged by the offering of Christ's body (Hebrews 10:10); we are sanctified by God the Father and preserved in Christ (Jude 1).

4. **Ephesians 2:6 (RSV)**
5. **2 Timothy 1:7 (GNB)**
6. **Hebrews 12:11 (GNB)**
7. **Psalms 42:1 (GNB)**
8. **Song of Songs 5:8 (AB)**
9. **Hebrews 12:1-25 (NRSV)**
10. **2 Peter 1:3 (NRSV)**
11. **James 1:2-4 (GNB)**
12. **Romans 5:3 (GNB)**
13. **Luke 4:14 (GNB)**
14. **Romans 8:11 (AB)**
15. **Isaiah 53:4 (AB)**

Chapter 7: Transformed into The Likeness of Christ

1. **Genesis 1:26 (AB)**
2. **Genesis 9:6 (AB)**
3. **Hebrews 10:1 (GNB)**
4. **1 Corinthians 15:45-47 (AB)**
5. **Ephesians 2:8-10 (KJV)**
6. **Colossians 1:15 (AB)**
7. **Colossians 3:10 (AB)**
8. **Romans 8:29 (AB)**
9. **2 Corinthians 3:18 (AB)**

Chapter 8: God Is Glorified by Your Transformation

1. These promises include: we receive proper teaching (Acts 24:24); we obtain grace and redemption (Romans 3:24); we have joy (Romans 5:11); there is no condemnation for those in Christ (Romans 8:1); we walk in the law of the Spirit of life (8:2); we are given the love of God in Christ (8:29); there is unity for Christians (Romans 12:5); we receive fullness and blessing (Romans 15:29); helpers and apostles are provided for disciples of Christ (Romans 16:3,7); we are approved in Christ (Romans 16:10); we undergo sanctification in Christ (1 Corinthians 1:2); we are made wise in Christ (1 Corinthians 4:10); we obtain a new life in Christ (1 Corinthians 4:17); we are given hope in Christ and are made alive in Christ (1 Corinthians 15:19,23); we triumph in Christ (2 Corinthians 2:14); the veil concealing the Old Testament is removed in Christ (2 Corinthians 3:14); we are made new creatures in Christ (2 Corinthians 5:17); God, in Christ, is in the process of reconciling the world to Himself (2 Corinthians 5:19); there is divine simplicity in Christ that protects us from deception (2 Corinthians 11:3); there is liberty in Christ (Galatians 2:4); the covenant of God is in Christ (Galatians 3:17).
2. **1 John 5:20 (GNB)**

3. **Ephesians 1:3 (GNB)**
4. **Ephesians 1:10 (GNB)**
5. **Romans 8:20-21 (NRSV)**
6. **John 17:22-23 (RSV)**
7. God needs no one to give Him glory (Psalms 29:2) and Jesus has the glory of the Father, irrespective of human responses (Psalms 8:5). Conversely, man cannot obtain or give eternal glory by his own efforts (Proverbs 25:27): neither will God share His glory arbitrarily (Isaiah 42:8). God will only give His glory to the upright (Psalms 84:11).
8. **Isaiah 43:7 (GNB)**
9. Psalms 85:9; Psalms 79:9; Isaiah 46:13; Zechariah 12:10; Jeremiah 9:24
10. Hebrews 2:10
11. 2 Corinthians 4:14
12. Colossians 1:22
13. 2 Corinthians 11:2
14. **2 Corinthians 3:18 (NRSV)**
15. **Psalms 104:31 (KJV)**
16. **Ephesians 2:4-7 (NRSV)**

Chapter 9: Changed into His Image (In the Twinkling of An Eye)

1. **1 Corinthians 15:52 (KJV)**
2. **1 John 3:2 (GNB)**
3. **Luke 5:8 (GNB)**
4. **1 Corinthians 15:51-52 (GNB)**
5. **1 Thessalonians 4:15-17 (GNB)**
6. 1 Peter 2:9
7. **Isaiah 6:2-3 (GNB)**
8. It is vital that we understand that authority is only given in the Kingdom of God to love Him and to love His creation.
9. **Revelation 3:21 (RSV)**

10. **Daniel 7:18, 27 (RSV)**
11. **2 Timothy 2:11-12 (RSV)**
12. **1 John 5:4 (RSV)**
13. **Romans 5:17 (RSV)**
14. **Romans 8:37 (RSV)**
15. Romans 8:17
16. The word "overcome" (*nikao*) is used in its various forms at key points during the Book of Revelation. It is used both to encourage and exhort, as a repeated condition for receiving the various gifts and blessings stated in this last book of the Bible.
17. **1 Corinthians 15:55-56 (RSV)**
18. There are three main interpretations of the prophecies regarding the millennium (the thousand year reign of Christ on earth). The one you subscribe to will reflect your literal or metaphorical understanding of key passages and will determine your view of eschatology and the role of Israel in the End Times. I offer below very limited summaries of these three general interpretations:
    a) Pre-Millennialism. This term is used to describe the view of those who believe in a literal thousand year reign by Christ on this earth, in Jerusalem. The "Pre" indicates the belief that Christ's return will come before this thousand year period, with the final judgement coming at the end of this period. This interpretation relies on a literal interpretation of Revelation Chapter 20.
    b) Post-Millennialism. This refers to the belief that Christ will return after the millennium. Those who subscribe to this position do not believe that the thousand year period is a literal span of time. What is believed is that there is yet to come a period of time during which Christ will demonstrate His authority on this earth in a new and extraordinary manner.
    c) A-Millennialism. This interpretation would argue that the thousand year period – like all numbers in Revelation – is not to be taken literally. It is not a future event, this view would argue, it is actually happening now as it was begun at

Pentecost and will end with the return of Christ. Whichever view you have been taught will affect to some degree whether you agree with my argument in this Chapter. However, most of what I say is plainly stated in Scriptures.

19. **Revelation 22:3-4, 15a (RSV)**